How to Use Money

Published by
Lotus Press

How to Use Money

Philip J. Samuel

Lotus PRESS
4263/3, Ansari Road,
Darya Ganj, New Delhi- 110002

Lotus Press
4263/3, Ansari Road, Darya Ganj, New Delhi-110002
Ph.: 32903912, 23280047, E-mail: lotus_press@sify.com
www.lotuspress.co.in

How to Use Money

ISBN: 81-8382-017-4

Reprint: 2010

Published by: **Lotus Press**, New Delhi-110 002
Printed at: DD Offset Printing Press, Noida.

PREFACE

Money is a medium of exchange which acts as an intermediary market good. Without money, the production and exchange of anything but the most rudimentary goods and services is impossible. The way you spend your money today will determine what you have six months from now, a year from now, five years from now, or in your lifetime. You are responsible for the amount of money you earn and for the amount of money you spend.

Successful money managers control the way they spend their money. They use money to accomplish the things that are important to them. Good money managers manage their money rather than letting it dribble away from them. The ability to manage money has to be learned, developed, and practised on a daily basis.

This book has been written for financial managers and business students interested in the practice of money management. It provides guidelines and techniques for using money wisely. The topics discussed include: how to spend your money, how to use money for business, how to analyse your financial position, how to keep financial records, how to distribute money among employees, how to save your money, how to invest your money and how to make money.

Editor

Money is a medium of exchange which acts as an intermediary market good. Without money, the production and exchange of anything but the most rudimentary goods and services is impossible. The way you spend your money today will determine what you have six months from now, a year from now, five years from now, or in your lifetime. You are responsible for the amount of money you earn and for the amount of money you spend.

This book has been written for financial managers and business students interested in the practice of money management. It provides guidelines and techniques for using money wisely. The topics discussed include: how to spend your money, how to use money for business, how to analyse your financial position, how to keep financial records, how to distribute money among employees, how to save your money, how to invest your money and how to make money.

CONTENTS

1

WHAT IS MONEY?

Money is the universal key, it fits all locks. Money has made the division of labour possible. It has made specialisation possible. It has made the accumulation of wealth over periods which exceed a human lifetime possible. Perhaps most important of all, it has hugely advanced the potential for amicable interaction between people. To survive as such, and to prosper, a rational animal must exchange.

He or she has language, to exchange ideas, and money, to exchange the fruits of ideas. From that foundation, everything else we see around us has been built. Without language, the exchange of anything but the most rudimentary ideas is impossible. Without money, the production and exchange of anything but the most rudimentary goods and services is impossible.

Money is a medium of exchange. It ensures the success of exchange by being the one item on offer that is always acceptable. Money is necessary because human beings must exchange to live together in peace, and to prosper. Money must be a physical entity. Neither the "electronic" money of today nor the notes and coin which circulate as cash has any official or legal connection with Gold and Silver. But they once did, and most people think that they still do. As long as that situation persists, the modern monetary system will function.

One looks for the most tradeable good, the good which is in highest demand, the good that has begun to be accepted, not as an end in itself, but as a means to an end. Money is the good that people do not want to consume, but want to use to make further exchanges easier. Human beings have lived together for more than two million years. Money in its modern form - coin of fixed weight and denomination - came into use less than three thousand years ago. It took a long time to discover the physical good which best serves the purpose of a medium of exchange.

In separate places, under different cultures, all over the world, the concept of a "medium of exchange" grew. People noticed that some goods were easier to trade than others. And people also noticed that these "more tradeable goods" had similar properties:

1. They were durable.
2. They were easily divisible into larger or smaller amounts.
3. They were comparatively scarce, procuring them required effort.
4. They were "homogeneous". Every item of the commodity was exactly like every other item.
5. They were convenient. It was easy to carry enough around to made trades for other commodities.

Over time, a shorter and shorter list of commodities passed all these tests. These select commodities began to exhibit a sixth property, all important in the evolution of money. This short list of commodities had one thing in common with all other commodities. They were useful and commanded an exchange value in their own right. But because they were easier to trade than any other goods, they came to be perceived as having a value over and above their basic utility. They came to have a value as a "most (easily) tradeable good". They came to have a value as a medium of exchange. Once this value became widely recognised, the commodity in question was no longer "consumed" for any but the most vital purposes. Instead, it was used in exchange. It had become a money.

INTRINSIC VALUE

In economics, there is no such thing as "intrinsic" value. This is true for the simple reason that value does not reside in the atoms, molecules, chemical composition, or structure of an economic good. It resides, always, in the MIND of the individual perceiving the good. When looking to acquire an economic good, an individual must decide how much time, or effort, or other economic goods he or she is willing to offer in exchange. That decision determines the value of that economic good, at that particular time, to that unique individual.

This is a crucial distinction. Value is not in what is beheld, it is in the eye (and mind) of the beholder. The reason why some goods evolve into money while most others do not has nothing to do with the "intrinsic value" of the goods so favoured. It is because a large number of individuals have realised that goods used as money have a unique usefulness. Unlike all other goods, they can be exchanged easily, and at any time, for anything.

1.1. FUNCTIONS OF MONEY

1.1.1. A Medium of Exchange

This simply means if you can use it to buy or otherwise obtain goods or services that you need or want, it's money. The simplest form of exchange is barter, where people or companies trade goods or services of roughly equivalent value with no money changing hands. When barter is inconvenient, an object may be used to represent value. That object is money! It has been many things: grain; cattle; shells; salt; precious stones and metals; pieces of paper; and bits and bytes of data stored on a computer or a smart card. The only requirement for this function is that the two (or more) parties accept the value represented by the object, and use that object to buy and sell goods and services.

1.1.2. A Standard of Measurement

Money is a standard of measurement or measure of value. This is the function that can result in confusion about the legality of money relative to gold, silver or other standards that have been used at times throughout history. Currency and coin may be based on any commodity with intrinsic value and coins may be worth the value of the metals used to mint them. There's no requirement that this be so. This function only means that we use money to express what something is worth, such as that car is worth $20,000 or a candy bar costs $0.50. In Japan the car and the candy bar would be worth so many yen. In England the measurement would be in pounds, and so on around the world.

1.1.3. A Means of Payment

This function is very similar to medium of exchange, and they are often joined in definitions. There is a fine distinction in that money as a means of payment can be one step removed from the actual exchange for goods and services. If we buy something with a credit card, the money available to borrow is the medium of exchange. When we write a check or authorise an online transfer of funds to make the payment to the credit card issuer we've used money in its payment form. When a form of money is described as legal tender it is referring to this function of money, meaning that the currency, coin, or other form can be used to pay debts and taxes.

1.1.4. A Store of Value or Wealth.

This function results from the belief or trust that the form of money will retain value over time. Forms of money that have intrinsic value, such as gold, silver, salt or cattle, are easier to understand because they are tangible. It's important to note that these items can fluctuate in value, however, just as inflation can reduce the value of currencies that are not based on something with intrinsic value or book entry or electronic accounts that have no tangible form at all.

1.2. DIFFERENT KINDS OF MONEY

There are many kinds of money. The most recognisable are currency and coins. Dollar bills, pennies, nickels, dimes, quarters, etc. are part of everyday life. In the United States, we have coins and dollar bills that are minted and printed by the government to use for exchange. Although the value of the money cannot be absolutely "guaranteed" by the government, we have faith in it because our government takes measures to protect its value and to encourage its acceptance. Our currency was once backed by the government and could be traded for gold or silver. In those times, someone who doubted the value of money could trade it for gold or silver.

Today, there is not nearly enough gold and silver to trade for all of our money. We have decided that we do not need the gold standard because we, as a society, have faith in our money's value and faith in the government to protect the value of our money. As a matter of fact, much of the world has faith in the value of our money. Although different countries may have money of their own, the dollar is a common medium for exchange around the world.

Coins and currency account for a relatively small amount of total spending, but most individual transactions may be made with cash. Although many of our day-to-day exchanges can easily be accomplished with cash, most of our large purchases and those purchases that do not require immediate cash payment are made with other forms of money. The most widely used form of money for exchanges today is a *check*. Checking account balances make up a majority of the total supply of money.

A check is very simple to explain. A check is a note to your bank asking the bank to give some of the money in your account to another person or business. If the person you buy something from believes that you really do have enough funds in your account, she will take the check and deposit it into her account. With a check, you do not have to risk losing the currency and coins. You can write a check for various amounts and you can easily transport it from one place to another.

1.2.1. Checking Accounts

Having a checking account allows you to spend money from that account by writing checks. For simplicity, we will consider commercial banks, savings and loans, credit unions, *etc*, as banks. The bank may charge a small fee for helping you to protect and use your money. Some accounts have a set fee each month that pays for certain services. A $3 or $4 monthly fee may entitle you to limited check writing, check cashing, and simple banking services. A $10 or $12 fee may entitle you to write as many checks as you want, travelers checks at no charge, a discount on a safe deposit box and an ATM card.

Every bank has a different set of fees for different services. It pays to shop around to find the fee that will provide you with the services you want. Sometimes, if you keep a minimum amount of money in your account throughout the month, you may not have to pay a fee.

Opening a checking account is simple. You will give the bank your personal information, such as your Social Security Number, and you are all set. You have to be of legal age to have an account of your own. Parents or guardians can set up a Custodial Account for a minor. In financial transactions, your Social Security Number becomes an important piece of identification.

If a purchase is a large one, you may not want to carry that amount of cash. If you are not sure how much you will spend, a check can be written for various amounts. If you lose a check, you do not lose the "money" in the bank. If someone else finds your check and "passes" it, you may have some problems, but you are protected by the laws that govern banks.

If the person you want to give your money to is far away, mailing a check is much more convenient. It is not a good idea to send cash in the mail. One really good thing about using a check is that the canceled check is lasting proof of your payment. Having a checking account may cost you a little more but the convenience may be well worth it. Most of the time the money in your account is insured. If something happens to the bank, you won't lose your money. Look at the door of the bank; if it says "FDIC Insured," your account is safe. FDIC stands for Federal Deposit Insurance Corporation. Other financial institutions may have similar insurance protection.

1.2.1.1. *Advantages and disadvantages of checks*

Checks are easily transported, can be written for any amount, and are widely accepted. Writing a check is like writing a note to your bank, asking them to give someone your money. This assumes that you have money on deposit in your account. Checks are relatively safe. If you destroy or lose one, you usually do not have a problem. Your canceled check is a permanent record of your payment.

As a tool for purchases, checks sound almost too good to be true. But, all of these advantages come with a cost. When you use cash, no one has to "process" the money. Whoever receives it then spends or saves it. Each check has to be sent from the payee's bank to the payer's bank. Bookkeeping transactions subtract money from one account and put it into another. All of this takes some physical effort and machines. Banks typically charge a fee to provide this service. For this fee, you get the convenience and the safety. Some will waive the fee for certain groups or those who keep a specified minimum amount in their account.

Another potential problem is if someone is tempted to write a check without an adequate balance in the account. "Bounced" checks cause problems, both for those who write them and those who accept them.

1.2.2. ATM's

Many people do their "banking" at the automatic teller machine (ATM) or "cash machine." ATMs are convenient ways to withdraw cash from an account or to make a deposit. Again, like checking accounts, some charge fees for transactions and some do not. Each bank will have its own rules for ATMs. When you apply for a check cashing or ATM card, ask about the fees and restrictions. While

ATMs are convenient, they may be a costly way of accessing your money.

Many banks charge fees if you use their cards in ATMs that are owned by other banks. Sometimes, the owner of the ATM will charge a fee if you do not have an account with that bank. It is possible that both banks will charge your account a fee. When choosing a bank, this may be an important consideration. You can also look for "no fee" ATMs. Even if you use a "no fee" machine, your bank may still charge you a fee. If you are not clear about the fees your bank charges, call the bank and ask.

1.2.2.1. Credit cards

Another way to make purchases is to use a credit card. When you use a credit card, you use an identification card to create a short-term "loan." The merchant creates a loan to you from the credit card company. The bank transfers money to the merchant's account. You, of course, have to pay the bill when your statement arrives. Credit cards are invaluable while traveling for car rentals, hotel reservations and safety. They are convenient and some types of cards are widely accepted.

1.2.2.2. Debit cards

The difference between a debit card and a credit card is that when you use a debit card, the amount is taken directly from your checking or savings account. With a credit card, you will usually have a grace period, a time within which you can pay the balance without additional cost. Debit cards are similar to writing a check.

Credit cards are widely accepted. Many merchants limit the amount of a debit card transaction. Typically, you will not be able to make a large purchase with a debit card. Another option is a check card issued by your bank that is processed just like a check.

All credit card agreements are different. Consumers should read their credit card agreements very carefully to understand the costs and benefits, and their rights and responsibilities. Credit cards are fairly safe to use. Even if someone illegally uses your credit card number and you report the card stolen or lost; you will not be responsible for the purchases over a total of fifty dollars. Credit cards have some real advantages. You do not have to carry large sums of cash. You can make purchases in almost any amount, but some merchants limit very small purchases to a minimum amount, such as twenty dollars. If a credit card is lost, it is easily replaced by contacting the bank or company. Your credit card receipt is a detailed record of your purchases. This helps with budgeting and for returns or refunds.

Credit cards do not come cheaply. Many have an annual fee. Annual fees vary greatly. Most of the time, if you pay off the total balance of your monthly bill, you will not owe interest. There may be exceptions for cash advances and certain specified conditions. Always read this part of the credit card agreement very carefully. If you do not pay the entire balance, you will owe interest. The interest is determined by multiplying a stated interest rate by the remaining balance. Shopping for a credit card, look for:

1. A card without an annual fee or a low annual fee. Annual fees vary greatly. With higher fee cards, such as "gold cards," you may receive additional services. Watch out for those that charge no fee for the first year only. After the first year, your fee may be considerably higher.

2. A low annual percentage rate (APR). First, be sure that the interest rate is not just for the first few months. Some card providers will give you a very low interest rate in the beginning that will increase

over time or if you do not make the required payments. If you plan to carry a balance, a low interest rate is very important.

3. A long grace period. Grace periods vary greatly from one card to another. The longer the grace period, the longer the amount of time between billing cycles. A card with a short grace period may require two payments within some months.
4. Watch out for hidden charges or extra charges for things like going over your credit limit, late payments or cash advances. When some companies give cards to people with poor credit records, they very often have high fees. Some credit cards have a minimum interest charge each month.

Read the credit card application very carefully. If you have question, call the customer service number on the application or your bill. If you do not like the conditions of you card, you can shop for a new one, but you will still have to pay the balance and fees on the old one. The type of card you get may depend on your spending habits. If you plan to pay off your purchases each month, choose a card with no annual fee. Do not worry so much about the interest rate.

If you plan to carry a balance, the interest rate is much more important. A longer grace period may be desirable, but that card may have a higher interest rate. Read the application carefully. Some cards offer premiums, a contest entry, or a percentage of your interest paid to a charity or directly back to you. All of these may come with some cost.

It is very easy to carry a large unpaid balance on a credit card. The smaller your payment, the more money you have to buy more things, right? Wrong! If you make only the minimum payments each month, you may end up paying as much as twice the original price. A $1,000 charge paid with the monthly minimum payment may take several years to pay off and may end up costing double the original amount.

If you send it through the mail, make sure that you allow enough days for your payment to get to the company. Even though you mailed it a few days earlier, it may take a few days more to get there. Some banks allow direct transfers from their customers' savings or checking accounts to make their credit card payments.

1.2.3. Other Options of Payment

Money orders, cashier's checks, and traveler's checks are similar methods of payment. In each case you are purchasing a check from a third party, possibly a bank or a store. People are more likely to accept these methods than a personal check. Traveler's checks are usually accepted like cash in foreign countries. A bank guarantees a cashier's check.

The provider guarantees a money order. If you have had problems paying bills in the past, a merchant might require you to use a money order, a cashier's check or cash. Accepting these forms of money is less risky for the merchant. The problem with these forms of money is that they almost always require an extra fee to process. Be sure to ask your bank if cashier's checks, money orders, or traveler's check fees are included in your monthly account fee.

A relatively new option is a money market mutual fund account. In this type of account, you own shares of an account that invests assets in various government and private securities. A money market account usually provides a slightly higher interest rate and is relatively safe. Many money market funds will allow you to deposit any amount, but limit the amount, which can be withdrawn.

2

HOW TO SPEND MY MONEY WISELY

In a perfect world, we would all avoid too much credit card debt and would never have to deal with the desperation of being unable to meet our credit card payment obligations.

We'd never know the frustration of not being able to afford what we really want because every extra cent has to go towards keeping up with the minimum payments on our credit cards. But this isn't a perfect world, and unfortunately these distressing situations are the norm for many people.

If you find yourself in this position, or headed there, take control of your spending now. Don't wait until your situation is so dire that you have few options available to you. An important aspect of debt that is not always addressed is why you got too deeply into debt in the first place. Why did you keep charging items you couldn't afford? Why did you feel the urge to use those little plastic cards for things that weren't necessary, even when you began to struggle to make the payments? What causes your compulsive shopping?

Facing the factors that give you the urge to splurge can be uncomfortable, but if you don't face them, you may never get control of your spending and your debt. If you're always trying to pay off yesterday's purchases, many of which have long since worn out or been forgotten, how will you acquire the things you truly want for tomorrow?

One negative aspect of using credit cards instead of cash is that you don't feel like you're spending real money. The pleasant feelings you experience when you purchase the item are disconnected from the unpleasant or painful feelings of making the payment when you get the credit card statement.

Studies show that most people are much less likely to buy, or less willing to spend as much, when paying with cash as opposed to credit cards. Try leaving your credit cards at home. Pay with cash, check, or a debit card. To really get control of your spending and your credit card debt, you need to examine what money means to you. Make an effort to notice how you interact with money and what beliefs and attitudes you have about money. Studies also show that people with low self-esteem engage in more impulse spending and buying things they don't need.

Remind yourself daily that money or a lack of it doesn't determine who you are. Your worth as a person has nothing to do with how much money you have. Once you truly believe this, and money is no longer connected to your sense of self-worth, you open up the psychological barriers that were keeping you from wisely handling the money you do have and limiting your ability to make more.

Right now, your unconscious limiting beliefs may be keeping you from being financially successful, but as you begin to build up your feelings of self-worth and develop a positive attitude about yourself and about money, you'll attract positive things into your life. As you do so, you'll feel less of a need to generate positive feelings by purchasing things, and you'll find it easier to stop buying items you don't really need.

There are hundreds of books, magazine articles, and Internet web sites about getting rid of credit card debt. Some of them offer sound advice about the psychological aspects of money and spending that you'd do well to consider. If psychological factors influence your spending, credit reduction programs are like using perfume to cover body odor: they will treat only the symptoms, not the root cause. Working on the psychological aspects while taking steps to reduce debt will greatly increase your chances of long-term success.

2.1. MONEY SPENDING PSYCHOLOGY

2.1.1. Avoid Spending Money Unnecessarily

Here are ten ways to avoid spending money unnecessarily.

1. Develop a budget for each department.
2. Develop a list of what employees are allowed to purchase.
3. Know how much cash you have in the bank every day.
4. Read and approve each expense.
5. Stay on top of and try to collect as quickly as possible your accounts receivable.
6. Extend your accounts payable.
7. Barter for services and products.
8. Only buy things you absolutely need.
9. Ask every vendor for advice on how to save money on products you purchase from them.
10. Put out a bounty on internal savings by rewarding employees with 10 percent of whatever money they can save the company.

Management must be diligent and well organised to ferret out unnecessary expenditures. The following is a list of unnecessary expense items that various clients of mine cut to save money.

Magazine Subscriptions: A client of mine once ran a company that had thirty employees and sixty-seven magazine subscriptions. Some people bought the same magazine twice. When she questioned them why they needed duplicate subscriptions, they stared at the floor and said so they wouldn't have to carry the extra paper in their briefcase. There are so many free subscription magazines available that this is one area you can save a nice amount of money. The company in this example was spending over $5,000 a year in magazine subscriptions, yet they couldn't afford to buy some much needed software and computers, which would pay for themselves by increasing productivity.

Telephone: The competition is so fierce that a company can always save money in this area, regardless of usage. One of my clients was paying fifteen cents a minute for long-distance charges from one of the top long-distance companies. He asked his controller to send out for bid their telephone bill. The result was a smaller company gave them a rate of nine cents, which translated into 40 percent savings; in this case the company saved $12,000 over the course of a year.

Mobile Telephone: This is an area that is widely abused, but usually unintentionally. A prudent client of mine told her employees that the company will only pay for calls to customers and prospects to tell them that they are running late or for some other emergency. As of the writing of this book, all the usage rates are basically the same, so the only way to save money is to instill discipline.

Leasing Companies: Most companies can't afford to buy all of the equipment they need to operate, so they lease equipment. Leasing is a very expensive form of financing. Shop around and look closely at three things before signing a lease: the rate of interest you are being charged, how much insurance they want you to carry or buy to protect their investment, and late penalties. Late penalties can sometimes cost as much as the lease itself. One of my clients decided to borrow money from his retirement plan, which he swore he would never do, and bought out the leasing contract he had signed because the interest rate he could pay himself was cheaper.

Insurance: Every type of insurance policy should be reviewed and put out for quote each year. Insurers who have to pay out a lot of money to cover liabilities end up having to raise everyone's rates, even those who had no claim. Therefore, putting your insurance out for bid each year can guarantee the company paying the lowest premiums. If your company files none or just a few claims, another insurer will be glad to add your company to their pool and lower your premiums for lowering their risk.

Service Contracts: Service contracts usually aren't worth the money with the exception of copier service contracts. All of my client's experiences are that photocopiers breakdown often, and the service charges are usually exorbitant.

Memberships: Only keep memberships in organisations that have the potential to bring you business. Also, the only people who should be members initially are company salespeople. Watch out for duplicate organisational memberships and make sure someone is responsible for being the liaison between the company and the organisation. Many of my clients who were in financial trouble called organisations they wanted to join and asked them for reduced rates or requested to pay on a monthly basis. My clients told me it was rare they were refused this request.

Advertising: Unless the company is in retail, minimise or eliminate advertising. A client of mine who ran a large retail mall decided to eliminate advertising; the percentage of shoppers dropped by half within two weeks. One client of mine employed a simple advertising tracking system. He used the same coupon in each publication in which he advertised, but put a number in the corner of the ad to indicate which publication the ad came from. Once these coupons came back, my client was able to know which publications provided the best responses and was able to eliminate advertising in those publications whose responses were low or nonexistent.

Charity: Companies can be overwhelmed with solicitations from worthwhile causes. Unfortunately, management has to restrain itself and eliminate all but those important to one or two big clients. In a turnaround situation, even charity has to have a return on investment.

Business Supplies: Buy only what is needed and try to purchase things on sale. Have one person responsible for the supply closet; any person who wants a supply item must sign for it. This will give you valuable information on usage and who is using certain items. One of my clients found that one person was using a lot of expensive computer disks. Their manager said they had to backup a project that required a lot of memory, and they could save the company a lot of money by erasing old disks used for former clients. My client asked why they weren't doing this already, and the manager said it was just a past policy of the former president to save everything. This requires a judgment call, but most times its best to reuse what you have unless you need to keep information for legal and/or contractual reasons.

Computers: Depending on the type of business you are in, you might not need a state-of-the-art computer system. Try upgrading what you have and make sure all equipment is being used to its fullest capabilities. One client's employees were so attuned to the company's financial situation that they started swapping parts out of old computers and reusing them. This saved the company a lot of money.

Travel: There are certain rules of travel people should follow. Never fly first class, unless the employee wants to pay the difference or has frequent flyer miles to cover the cost. If there are two airports within an hour to and hour and a half drive time, check which one offers the best rate. Flying to San Francisco from Philadelphia is 50 to 80 percent higher than flying out of Baltimore.

When attending a convention, always ask for the corporate rate at the hotel; never stay at the hotel booked by the convention. Usually hotels nearby a convention offer rates 20 to 50 percent below what a guest would have to pay for the convenience of staying in the convention's hotel. When visiting a Fortune 500 client, ask them for the hotel they use and if you can use their corporate rate. The savings can be significant.

When a company is in crisis mode, management needs to have every line item that represents $1,000 or more on a spreadsheet so managers can see where all of the company's money is going. Below is a sample of how to review expenses

2.1.2. Spending Money Wisely

While the old axiom of you have to spend money to make money is certainly true, it isn't just simply the act of spending money that creates earnings. Although it's necessary to purchase equipment and supplies to perform the services we sell, it seems obvious that the less we spend for these supply items, the greater our profits will be. Some of the things that affect this important part of business.

2.1.2.1. *Price and Value*

Sometimes the lowest price does not equal the best value. Buying the least expensive equipment or chemistry may actually end up costing you more. Make sure you understand why the product is less expensive. If it makes you work slower because it is less efficient than the more expensive version, the extra time might be more costly than the price difference. Remember, labor is your greatest expense in a service company and even a small labor savings is valuable. Sometimes chemistry is priced lower because it's less concentrated; thus, making the cost for the diluted ready-to-use product higher. Evaluate your equipment and chemicals in terms of productivity and not only on price.

2.1.2.2. *Volume of Purchases*

Buying a single gallon of cleaning agent will certainly have less immediate impact on cash flow than buying a case. However, if you use the product in a reasonable time period, then the price per gallon will be less in the case purchase than the individual gallon price. Added to this is the cost of several trips to the supplier or several shipments as opposed to one. The key is to balance the purchase with the rate of use.

The ideal scenario is to run out of product the day the new supplies arrive. This "just in time" philosophy has some dangers attached. Sometimes, supplier availability and/or lead time is not as expected. Occasionally, business has unexpected surges and your rate of consumption is faster than expected. There are even times when "Murphy's Law" takes over and things just go wrong without prior warning. While some of these challenges cannot be anticipated, many can be avoided by building a cushion into your ordering system.

First, determine the normal lead time for supply orders to arrive. Next, using your expected rate of usage, determine the latest you can order for "just in time" needs. Back up from there, about half the lead time, and that's your reorder point. Each time your supplies reach the level equal to 1-1/2 the amount needed during the normal reorder period, place your order for the next amount. Any seasonal fluctuation in business must be taken into consideration. You don't want to stockpile supplies in the slow season, and you certainly don't want to run out in the busy season. Rush shipments from suppliers can be costly.

2.1.2.3. *Planned Purchases*

Even the best equipment has an effective life span. Proper maintenance and care can increase its life, but all equipment eventually wears out or becomes obsolete. Keep commonly needed repair and replacement parts in stock and initiate a planned preventive maintenance program to minimise downtime. Broken down equipment costs three ways:

1. Cost of repairs.
2. Lost production.
3. Loss of reputation and customer trust.

Not being able to get the job done when promised may be the biggest cost of all in the long run.

Start an equipment account that is tied to production volume. For example, you could put 3% of the gross amount produced by a truckmount into the equipment account each month. A truck producing Rs. 500,000 per month would build the account at a rate of Rs, 15,000 per month, or Rs. 180,000 per year, or Rs. 1800,000 in 10 years (plus interest if it is the right kind of account). Money is available for "emergency" repairs, and when the time comes to purchase new equipment or replace old machines, the equipment account is there to help reduce the purchase price and reduce the amount paid in finance charges.

The reason it should be on a percentage is that the bigger your business, the more equipment costs you will have. Also, the bigger the business, the greater the account becomes. If your business plan calls for a sharp growth, don't forget to budget in the cost of good equipment to accomplish the growth. Arrange the financing with your banker before going to the supplier.

3

MONEY AND BUSINESS

There is no basic measure for gauging an owner's equity stake compared to investors' equity in the firm. But there are two very important concepts about business financing that do apply to the general topic of owners' equity. When term sheet proposals are being circulated along with a company's executive summary, investors always focus their initial attention on four major areas:

1. What is the product or service concept, and how is it differentiated from the competition?
2. How large is the potential market for this product or service?
3. Who on the management team will drive the business strategy forward?
4. What do the business model and the financial structure look like? This fourth area examines the way the company makes money, as well as the debt-equity arrangement that capitalises the assets that will be employed to achieve success with that model.

When outside investors see that the company founders have already invested significant time into the business, that's well-received. But sweat-equity alone is not enough to persuade investors to fund the deal. In addition to plenty of hours invested working in the business, the owners must also be equity investors with money at risk—otherwise, capital providers view the level of commitment as being less than desirable.

The second important concept is the form of the founders' capital commitment to the company. Some entrepreneurs will provide a loan to their new venture, and it may even be secured by fixed assets purchased with those funds. This is less positive than if the founding team has stock in the firm. The time frame for the company to pay off a loan can also be a concern to outside investors.

If the owners have a provision to pay themselves back within a year or 18 months, the priority of payment sends a signal to outside capital providers that the owners want to be sure to cover their own personal financial positions first, and this can cause concern. Outside investors would much rather see the owners in a side-by-side position with them, where everyone has an equity stake and no one is getting priority of payments from operating cash flow.

Equity stakes for the founders always look better than short-term and/or secured loans to the company. When outside investors do co-invest with the entrepreneur, the deal will go much more smoothly if owners and founders are equity investors and they're both in the same class of securities. For example, outside capital providers will frown on the situation where the founders have preferred stock, while investors have lower-priority common stock. The best way to put these two concepts together is to understand the perceived risk of the venture.

Investors will always look for ways to mitigate certain risk exposure in order to reduce the potential for capital loss. Some companies pursue financing strategies that are entirely based on using "other people's money" to grow the firm. That makes sense when additional funds needed for expansion come in from outside investors, as long as those are in addition to the founders' initial capital invested.

But when working with outside funding sources, be sure they understand clearly your commitment to the venture—and the reduced risk perception—by bearing some of the company risks through your own equity investment. There are so many other line items to be negotiated in doing a funding deal that the question of an owner's equity participation should not be one of them.

3.1. BUSINESS PLAN

A guide to writing a business plan, which can be a major factor in securing loans and investments for businesses. The guide covers what should be included in the plan, as well as what information should be placed in each section of it. Every day, thousands of people try to get their hopes and dreams to take flight. Would-be small business owners desperately seek investors, lenders, and people who have faith in their visions, all the while established businesses try to expand their horizons into new markets.

Some of them make it; more of them don't. It's not necessarily because they have an inferior product or that their goals aren't reachable...often, they simply don't have their ideas organised in a way that the people who are funding the project can follow. Without the money, the greatest ideas won't go anywhere. The best way to show potential investors or lenders exactly what you have in mind with a project or business is to draft a business plan that you can present to them.

A business plan is a written account of what you hope to accomplish, how much it will cost, and who else in the area is already doing the same thing. It organises the whole of the project in a way that can be easily referenced and understood by those who aren't working intimately with the project itself.

How much information should be included in a business plan? Strictly speaking, you can include as much or as little as you want, but as a general rule you want your plan to contain both the up and down sides of what you're wanting to do while giving a general view of how much everything will cost as well as an estimate of how much money will be made. The plan should be around 40 – 50 pages long; if it goes much longer then you might lose your readers in details and jargon, and if it's much shorter then there's a good chance that you left something out. When writing your business plan, use the following guide to make sure that you tell the story that you want to tell to the people holding the pursestrings.

3.1.1. Executive Summary

The executive summary is one of the most important parts of your business plan; it should be the first thing in the plan, but should be written last so that you don't leave out anything on the pages that follow it. Write a 1 – 2 page overview of the plan as a whole.

3.1.2. Industrial Analysis

When dealing with bankers and investors, there's a good chance that they don't know much about the industry that your business will be competing in. Even if they do, assume that they don't and write a summary of the industry as a whole. Include industry opportunities, recent changes, industry leaders, and what the leaders of the industry did to get where they are today.

3.1.3. Market Analysis

More specific than the industrial analysis, the market

analysis talks about what's going on in the industry specific to the area where you'll be working. Include market opportunities, an overview of the competition, how you're different from the competition, and what plans you have to succeed against them.

3.1.4. Business Description

Once you've given an overview of both your industry as a whole and the local market, it's time to start getting specific. Describe your business, who owns it, how long you've been in business, the short-term and long-term goals that you have for the business, and exactly what you need the money for (expansion, marketing, debt-reduction, equipment, start-up costs, etc.)

3.1.5. Competition Description

Going back to the competition mentioned in the market analysis, give a basic description of how your business is better than they are. List the strengths of your competition as well as their weaknesses, and tell why you think you'll be able to succeed against them.

3.1.6. Marketing Plan

This is where you start to show how you plan on making the lenders or investors their money back. Describe what plans you have for marketing your products or services, who you are likely to have as customers (and already have, if writing the plan for an existing company), why new customers are likely to buy from you, the pricing strategy that you plan to use, the distribution you use for any products that you make, and the general plans that you have for promoting your business.

3.1.7. Operations

If your business is a product-based business, then this is one of the most important sections of the entire business plan; describe all of your equipment and how it works, as well as the manufacturing processes that you use. For product based or service-based businesses, you should include information about what departments exist within your business, how the business is run as a whole, and any plans that you have for possible expansion.

3.1.8. Organisation

This is the area where you describe the people who'll be running the show with the investors' money. Write a brief paragraph about all of your managers and owners, giving the readers an idea of their expertise and background. You should also make organisational charts to show how your labor force is divided, and include plans and policies for the addition and subtraction of employees.

3.1.9. Funding Needs

This is where you detail the total amount of money needed (as well as any lesser amounts that can be used while still getting the job done), how that money will be used (be it for buildings, equipment, hiring, capital, marketing, etc.), and a description of why the plan that you have for the money is the right way that it should be used. While much of the rest of the plan is used to supply information.

3.1.10. Financial Statements

For established businesses, include any past financial statements as well as income projections for the next five years. Start-ups should simply create the five-year projections; you should do balance sheets, income statements, and five years of cash flow with monthly projections for the first three years and then quarterly projections for the remaining two.

3.1.11. Appendix

The appendix should hold any information that's important, but didn't really need to be included in the main plan. This could include awards you or your company have won, maps of proposed sites, sample marketing literature, management resumes, or details of recent contracts or clients.

3.2. BUSINESS LOANS

A loan is based on a simple idea: someone gives you money and you promise to pay it back, usually with interest. Loans are so common that you probably are familiar with the mechanics, but nevertheless it makes sense to review the basics. The success or failure of your business can hinge on borrowing money sensibly: you want to borrow enough that your company can reach its potential but not so much that you have severe difficulty paying it back.

3.2.1. Lenders

You have many options when looking a loan for your business. For small ventures, friends and family members are sometimes willing to help. For sophisticated or mid-sized businesses, banks, credit unions, and savings and loans may be willing to lend you money.

3.2.2. Promissory Note

A lender will almost always want you to sign a written

promissory note — a paper that says, in effect, "I promise to pay you $XXX plus interest of XX%." While a friend or relative may be willing to lend you money on a handshake, this is a bad idea for both of you. It's always a better business practice to put the loan in writing, and to state a specific interest rate and repayment plan. Otherwise, you open the door to unfortunate misunderstandings that can chill your relationship. Also, you want to have documentation of the loan's terms in case the IRS decides to audit your business.

3.2.3. Interest

State usury laws prevent lenders from charging illegally high interest on loans. As a general rule, a lender can safely charge you interest of up to 10% per year and not have to worry about violating this usury law. However, there's a lot of variation in usury laws from state to state, and different rules apply to commercial lenders and private lenders, so you should check your state's law if you're concerned. If your corporation is taking a loan from a shareholder (including yourself), make sure the interest rate is not too low — the IRS likes to see loans that are commercially reasonable. Otherwise, the IRS might consider the loan as a capital investment by the shareholder and treat the loan repayments as dividend payments to the shareholder.

3.2.4. Security Interests

Many lenders will require you to put up valuable property that they can sell to collect their money if you don't make your loan payments. For example, a lender may take a second mortgage or deed of trust on your house, or ask for a security interest or lien on your business's equipment, inventory, or accounts receivable.

3.2.5. Personal Liability

Depending on how your business is organised, if you don't make good on your repayment commitment, a lender has the right to sue you individually or sue your business entity. If the lender sues you individually, it can take your personal assets to satisfy the loan. If the lender sues your business entity, it can take the business's assets.

3.2.6. Cosigners, Guarantors, and Personal Guarantees

A lender may also require that someone cosign or guarantee the loan. That means the lender will have two people rather than one to collect from if you don't make your payments. When asking friends or relatives to cosign or guarantee a promissory note, be sure they understand that they're risking their personal assets if you don't repay the loan.

If you've organised your business as a limited liability entity, such as a corporation or an LLC, the lender will probably ask you — the business owner — to personally guarantee the loan and/or pledge your personal assets to guarantee repayment. Be aware that guaranteeing or personally cosigning your business's loan circumvents your limited liability status.

All of your separate property, and either half or all of any property you jointly own with a spouse could eventually be seized if you default on the loan. Finally, if you're married, the lender may insist that your spouse cosign the promissory note. If your spouse cosigns the loan, not only is your jointly owned property completely at risk for this joint debt, but also any assets that your spouse owns separately—a house, for example, or a bank account. What's more, if your spouse has a job, his or her earnings will be subject to garnishment if the lender sues and gets a judgment against the two of you.

3.3. RAISING MONEY FOR BUSINESS

3.3.1. Investments

To raise money for your new business, you must decide whether you want to borrow money or sell ownership interests to equity investors. Often, you may not have many options — the person with money to lend or invest will obviously have a lot to say about it. But you should understand the pros and cons of choosing one over the other.

3.3.2. Borrowing Money

Borrowing money to fund your business has many advantages. Often, you'll borrow this money from a friend or family member, but if you're lucky, you may be able to borrow from a commercial lender too.

The main advantage of borrowing money is that, while the lender will charge you interest for using the money, the lender won't have any say in how you run or manage your business. More importantly, a lender won't be entitled to any of the profits you make; all you have to do is to repay the loan on time.

In addition, you can typically deduct the interest payments (but not principal repayments) as a business expense. If you can borrow money from a friend or family member, you'll typically pay a lower rate of interest than if you borrow the money from a commercial lender, and you can avoid paying the loan fees commercial lenders tend to charge. As an added bonus, you may be able to negotiate more flexible repayment terms than a commercial lender would permit.

If you borrow money, you may be committing your business to a fairly large business expense. You may have to make loan payments when your need for cash is greatest. And if you have problems paying the loan back or keeping up with the payments, you can ruin your relationship with family or friends. If you borrow from a commercial lender, the lender may require you to pledge property as security for the loan.

If you pledge business property as security for the loan, and your business slows down and you can't make loan payments, you may lose these valuable assets just when you need them most. Worse, if you pledge personal assets, such as your house or stock portfolio, you risk losing them to pay a business debt. Even if you organise your business as a corporation or a limited liability company, almost all commercial lenders will require you, as the owner of a new or small business, to personally guarantee the loan and/or to pledge personal assets to cover the loan, which wipes out this limited liability.

3.3.3. Accepting Investments

If you have friends, family, or other people who want to invest in your business outright (become part-owners) instead of simply lending you money, you can raise money for your small business this way too. However, allowing people (called equity investors) to own part of your business comes with its own set of advantages and disadvantages.

Advantages of equity investors: First, there's a good practical reason to take investments: Raising money through equity investors allows you to use your cash to pay business start-up expenses rather than large loan payments. And unlike a loan, if your business loses money or goes broke, you probably won't have to repay your investors their initial investment.

As long as you've thoroughly disclosed the risks involved in your business, your investors should understand and accept that they are not guaranteed to get their money back. Further, investors often have business experience and can offer you valuable advice, moral support, and assistance.

Disadvantages of Equity Investors: On the downside, equity investors usually end up taking a larger share of your business's profits than a bank or other lender. In addition, your investors will be co-owners, and they have a legal right to be informed about all significant business events, as well as a right to ethical management. Your co-owners can (and probably will) sue you if they feel you are compromising their rights. This means you always have a responsibility to take your investors' interests into account when you make business decisions, even if it's not what's best for you.

In some circumstances, your investors may be considered passive investors and their investment interests "securities." Dealing with securities creates a lot of paperwork, starting with securities registration, and brings a host of other legal requirements down on your head. However, not all offerings of securities must be registered with the federal and state securities exchange commissions. The following are exempted:

1. Private offerings to a limited number of persons or institutions.
2. Offerings of limited size.
3. Intrastate offerings.

3.4. GETTING A BUSINESS LOAN

Bankers and institutions that lend money are often overly cautious in making loans to small businesses because of their high failure rate. As a result, these institutions have developed a lot of knowledge about the success rate of small businesses, and they apply this knowledge when they approve and deny loans. For that reason, it makes sense to study their approach, even though it may seem discouraging at first glance.

3.4.1. Banker's Ideal

Bankers look for a loan applicant who meets these requirements:

1. For an existing business, a cash flow sufficient to make the loan payments.
2. For a new business, an owner who has a track record of profitably owning and operating the same sort of business.
3. For all businesses, an owner with financial reserves and personal collateral sufficient to solve the unexpected problems and fluctuations that affect all businesses.

Institutions who lend money are most comfortable with people so close to their ideal loan candidate that they don't need to borrow. However, to stay in business themselves, banks and other lenders must loan out the money deposited with them. To do this, they must lend to at least some people whose creditworthiness is less than perfect.

Your job is to show how your situation is similar to the banker's ideal. For instance, even if you haven't owned a successful business in the same field as your proposed new business, it can help if you have worked for, or preferably managed, such a business. Further away from a lender's ideal is the person who has sound experience managing one type of business, but proposes to start one in a different field.

3.5. SHORT-TERM LOAN SOLUTIONS

Can a business borrow some money for the short-term to

help cover expenses while building revenues? Yes, and the way to do this type of deal is to secure three or four investors to lend your business funds as part of an overall one-year to 18-month plan. The big picture is that this format is really a series of short-term loans perfectly sequenced to fit end to end. There are many companies who have used this successfully to keep cash flow flowing while they build and implement the firm's sales and marketing plan.

The first four or five monthly payments can actually be made from the proceeds of the loan, provided there is a successor loan set to kick in on the back-end of each credit extension. And owners should understand that each successive round of funding should be an increased level compared to the prior level. There are significant risks involved in pursuing this kind of a deal, but there are also some very attractive potential benefits that buy your company some time to get established in the market.

If the firm does not generate sales and any loan cannot be extended, and all the loan proceeds have already been spent, then the lender will foreclose on the principal and the owner(s) could be personally liable for repayment, or assets pledged as collateral could be seized to repay the principal. But these risks are manageable if the owners don't use all the funds at each access point and reserve a portion of the principal for monthly debt service and/or a "good faith" early principal portion repayment.

There are five basics that must be in place before you sit down with potential investors. If any of these items is not fully at the ready, it does not matter that the others are 100 percent in place. Investors will not give you credit for having four out of five of these items in proper shape. Rather, they will notice the one area that needs a lot of work. Your venture's portfolio of disclosure and readiness must be complete, with nothing missing across the board in these five areas. Five important areas are given below:

1. Have a final, airtight version of your business plan. The plan must be concise yet comprehensive in scope and provide enough details to satisfy all the questions that will no doubt be raised about your company's ability to accomplish its market objective.
2. Provide a personal financial statement of current income and past income (cash flow) for the past three to five years. As part of this personal financial disclosure, be prepared to demonstrate assets (home, stocks, pension funds, savings accounts) and liabilities (mortgage, car loans, credit card debts) in order to show a clear dollar value of your net worth. Also, in this personal disclosure, it is very important that the investors see that the lead entrepreneur and founding management team have some capital at risk as well in the venture. Asking others to back your vision and market strategy is especially difficult when you do not have a single dime exposed to the risks of loss that the investors' capital will be exposed to, should the funding deal close.
3. Make sure the management team is completely in place. If you cannot bring these key people to the meeting, have signed letters from them agreeing to take certain positions in the company. Include detailed resumes regarding their background, education and experience qualifying them to deliver tangible results in your new venture. Also, be sure your company has named a core board of directors to oversee operations, and leave one or

two seats available for the investors to fill or have their agents join on their behalf. Also put together a formal advisory board of individuals who will work with the lead entrepreneur on referrals and contacts as the venture moves forward.

Finally, have your attorney and accountant provide letters and documents about the venture, such as: articles of incorporation, investment letters, opening balance sheet and income statements, documentation on patents pending and other intellectual property and trademarks/copyrights in place or in process, and an initial capitalisation sheet outlining the founding team's stakes in the venture. If there are a lot of missing pieces, the investors will not invest at this juncture until those items are in place and secure.

4. Get both supply-side and demand-side documents together. For example, if you've already approached vendors about supplying your company with materials and supplies, and if you've opened up good negotiations on possible terms and discounts, bring letters from these firms to the meeting. The letters should be on their letterhead and should state that they're already working with you in these matters. You should have also opened up some preliminary discussions with some potential buyers of your product or service in the targeted market. In the same manner, you should also bring letters from these people stating that you are in negotiations about some contracts that your new venture will be able to fulfill once the capital is raised.
5. Make sure your product or service is already being used by someone or by a company, at least in its beta test form. Have a working model of the device,

or have a prototype of the product that the investors can touch and see in action. If it's a service, show how the pieces of the process are in place and how they are going to work together in delivering that service to your target clientele.

4

HOW TO ANALYSE MY FINANCIAL POSITION

Business owners who haven't been schooled in accounting often have a limited understanding of how financial analysis can help them manage their businesses effectively. Although you may be used to getting quarterly or annual financial statements from your accountant. Over the years, accountants and financial professionals have developed a number of systematic ways of arranging and comparing the financial facts about your business so that they can be used to make sound decisions about future actions. Tools for financial analysis are:

1. Financial statements, including the income statement, balance sheet, statement of changes in financial position, and statement of changes in owners' equity.
2. Business ratios that identify key relationships between financial data and allow you to monitor your liquidity, profitability, and efficiency.
3. Cost/volume/profit analysis, a way of determining the true cost to you of providing your product or service, and the optimal operation level for your business.

4.1. FINANCIAL STATEMENTS

If you want a clear understand of how your business is doing financially, and you want to be able to predict and plan for the future, a fairly thorough understanding of your financial statements is essential. A sound understanding of financial statements will help:

1. Identify unfavorable trends and tendencies in your business's operations (for example, the unhealthy buildup of inventory or accounts receivable) before the situation becomes critical.
2. Monitor your cash flow requirements on a timely basis, and identify financing needs early.
3. Monitor important indicators of financial health (for example, liquidity ratios, efficiency ratios, profitability ratios, and solvency ratios).
4. Monitor periodic increases and decreases in wealth (specifically, owners' or stockholders' equity).
5. Monitor your performance against your financial plan, if you have developed one.

There are four basic kinds of financial statements that can help you determine the present condition of your business. Here's a brief description of them:

1. The income statement, also referred to as a "profit and loss statement," "statement of incomes and losses," or "report of earnings," tells you or your investors:
   a. The income the business has earned during the accounting period.
   b. The costs or expenses that were incurred by the business during the period.
   c. The difference between the costs and incomes for the period, or net profit (or loss).

2. The balance sheet is a statement of a company's relative wealth or financial position at a given point in time. It shows assets, liabilities, and owners' equity.
3. The position statement, also known as the "statement of changes in financial position" or "sources and uses of cash," helps to explain how a company acquired its money and how it was spent.
4. The statement of changes in owners' equity is used to bridge the gap between the amount of owners' equity at the beginning of the period and the amount of their equity at the end of the period.
5. What to do with your financial statements contains a checklist of ways to look at the data to put it in perspective.
6. Common size financial statements provides an easy way to spot trends in your balance sheets and income statements over time is to convert the dollar amounts to percentages.

Keep in mind that your financial statements are only a starting point for analysis. Individual numbers aren't good or bad in themselves — you may have to dig for the reason behind any numbers that seem out of whack.

For instance, if your statements shows that your accounts receivable have trended significantly downward over the last few years, it could mean that you're collecting the accounts more aggressively (which is good), or it could mean that you're writing off accounts as uncollectible too soon (which is bad). The key is to use your statements to spot trends and anomalies, and then follow these up with further investigation.

4.1.1. Basic Rules for Financials

Finance is just as much a sport as football. The rules of

the finance game are called the generally accepted accounting principles (GAAP) and are set forth by the American Institute of Certified Public Accountants (AICPA) and the Financial Accounting Standards Board (FASB). GAAP includes numerous guidelines and conventions that help insure that reported financial information is accurate, objective, and reasonably consistent for all types of business, so that results from one business can be compared to those from another.

Most likely, your financial statements will be prepared by your accountant, who will follow the GAAP rules when creating them. Some investors or banks require that financial statements be prepared by a CPA because this gives the lender an extra measure of security — CPAs have proven that they have extensive knowledge of accounting, tax, and legal requirements by passing a difficult professional examination, and must build up their knowledge with continuing education. What's more, CPAs must adhere to certain professional ethics requirements or risk losing their licenses.

Even if you're not required to use a CPA by your bank, you may decide to have a CPA prepare your statements, particularly if you're planning to seek financing or investors in the near future. However, you can also opt to have a non-CPA accountant prepare your statements, or even to prepare your own financial statements. A number of software products are available that incorporate GAAP and make this job relatively simple, provided you understand the basic concepts we're about to explain to you.

A trial balance spreadsheet can be found in the Business Tools area. It is an Excel 4.0 spreadsheet template, so you can use the template as a starting point for your own trial balance. Another Business Tool is a sample balance sheet. It is an Excel 4.0 spreadsheet template, so you can use the template over again; you need to download it only once. Finally, you may also download a sample income statement. It is also an Excel 4.0 spreadsheet template, so you can use the template more than once.

Unless your bank needs to see them more frequently, many businesses request that the statements be prepared by their accountant every quarter. Some smaller businesses find that once a year (around tax time) is enough. However, if you have financial software at your fingertips, you may find it so easy to draw up provisional statements yourself that you do it monthly, or whenever you feel the need to get precise information on how your business is doing.

4.1.2. Balance Sheets

The balance sheet is a statement of your company's relative wealth or financial position at a given point in time. It's often referred to as a "snapshot" because it gives you a fairly clear picture of the business at that moment, but does not in itself reveal how the business arrived there or where it's going next. That's one reason why the balance sheet is not the whole story — you must also look at the information from each of the other financial statements to get the most benefit from the data.

Along with other financial information, balance sheet data is frequently analyzed and put into perspective through the construction of business and financial ratios. In many cases, ratios are constructed for each balance sheet (and income statement) for a number of years, so that you can make comparisons and spot important trends. The balance sheet consists of three categories of items: assets, liabilities, and stockholders' or owners' equity.

1. *Assets*: Assets are generally divided into two groups — current assets and fixed (long-term) assets. They

are usually presented in order of liquidity, with current assets (cash and those that will be converted to cash within one year) appearing first.

2. *Liabilities*: Liabilities are normally presented in order of their claim on the company's assets (i.e., liabilities due within one year are presented before liabilities due several years from now).
3. *Equity*: Stockholders' equity (or owner's equity or net worth) is presented properly when each class of ownership is presented with all its relevant information (for example, number of shares authorized, shares issued, shares outstanding, and par value). If retained earnings are restricted or appropriated, this also should be shown.

4.1.2.1. Improving Balance Sheet

Although steps can be taken just prior to the balance sheet date (generally, year end) to improve it, you should be aware of how your actions and decisions throughout the year affect the "balance sheet appearance" of your company that may be presented to outsiders.

Often, the individual balance sheet items can be improved to give a better-looking overall picture. For instance, cash balances often can be improved simply by retaining cash collected on receivables until after the balance sheet date, rather than promptly spending the money.

Another area to watch, if you manufacture goods, is inventory. Since finished goods are more easily converted to cash than are raw materials, and also have a higher value, converting more raw materials to finished goods before the balance sheet date looks better when presented in the financial statements. Whatever your business, you may want to hold off on writing off receivables as uncollectable bad debts, or writing down marketable securities to reflect a decline in value.

Sometimes year-end planning to reduce taxes may be in conflict with year-end planning to improve financial statements. This is because higher income looks good on your financial statements, but can cause you to pay more income tax. In such a case, you may have to choose between paying higher taxes to make your company's financial statements look better, or foregoing improved statements to reduce taxes. Depending on the business and its needs, lower tax payments are not always your best choice.

The fact that a business owner can take steps to improve the balance sheet's appearance illustrates one of the shortcomings of the statement. To the extent that it can be manipulated, it becomes less reliable as an indication of a business's true financial condition.

Besides improving the individual items shown on your balance sheet, you can also improve its appearance by improving your business ratios (or the relationship between certain items). To illustrate how you can do this, consider four key business ratios derived from balance sheet figures. Two deal with the liquidity of the business (current ratio and quick ratio) and two deal with the management of business debt (debt-to-equity and debt-to-assets ratios).

4.1.2.2. Income Statements

While the balance sheet is a financial snapshot, giving you a picture of the business's assets and liabilities on a single day at the end of the accounting period, the income statement shows you a summary of the flow of transactions your business has had over the entire accounting period. In other words, the income statement shows you what happened during the period between balance sheets.

The income statement, also referred to as a "profit and loss statement," "statement of incomes and losses," or "report of earnings," tells you or your investors:

1. The income the business has earned in the accounting period.
2. The costs or expenses that were incurred by the business during the period.
3. Your net profit — the difference between the costs and income for the period.

Three years' worth of income-statement data are normally presented, so that you can make comparisons and identify trends. The data consists of the following types of items:

1. Sales revenue.
2. Sales returns and allowances.
3. Other income.
4. Cost of goods sold.
5. Selling, general, and administrative expenses.
6. Depreciation and amortization expenses.
7. Interest expense.
8. Income taxes.

Using Income statement: As with the balance sheet, an in-depth knowledge of accounting is not necessary for you to make good use of the income statement data.

For example, you can use your income statement to determine sales trends. Are sales going up or down, or are they holding steady? If they're going up, are they going up at the rate you want or expect? Also, if you sell goods, you can use the income statement to monitor quality control. Look at your sales returns and allowances. If that number is rising, it may indicate that you have a problem with product quality.

Gross profit margin should be closely monitored to make sure that your business is operating at the same profitability levels as it grows. To find this margin, divide your gross profit by your sales for each of the years covered by the income statement. If the percentage is going down, it may indicate that you need to try to raise prices. Also, check out your selling expense. It should increase only in proportion to increases in sales. Disproportionate increases in selling expense should be followed up and corrected.

General and administrative expenses should also be closely watched. Increases in this area may mean that the company is getting too bureaucratic and is in line for some cost-cutting measures, or that equipment maintenance is too expensive and new equipment should be considered. Interest expense is an important measure of how your company is doing. If your interest expense is increasing rapidly as a percentage of sales or net income, you may be in the process of becoming overburdened with debt.

4.1.2.3. Changes in Position

The statement of changes in financial position provides data that are not explicitly present in the balance sheet or the income statement. This statement helps to explain how your company acquired its money and how it was spent. This statement can also help to identify financing needs, to identify cash drains, and to identify holes in the cash budgeting process. Use the statement of changes in financial position as a tool to analyze cash inflows and outflows. Also, use it as a starting point to forecast future cash flows and financing requirements.

Accounting standards give preparers of this statement quite a bit of flexibility in how they arrange and format the information. However, the Financial Accounting Standards Board has stated its intention that this statement should evolve into one whose focus is on cash and changes in cash. This position has been strongly endorsed by the Financial Executives Institute (FEI). As might be expected, more and more companies are using a cash focus for the statement of changes in financial position.

In fact, the statement is often called the "Sources and Uses of Cash Statement." The statement of changes in financial position should also include a supplement detailing the net changes in working capital. Specifically, this would include increases (or decreases) in accounts receivable, inventory, and accounts payable.

4.1.2.4. *Changes in Equity*

This type of financial statement is used to bridge the gap between the amount of equity the owners have in the business at the beginning of the accounting period and the amount of their equity at the end of the period. The income statement summarizes the revenues and expenses during the accounting period. The statement of changes in financial position is used to show the condition of accounts at the end of a particular period. The statement of changes in owners' equity does a bit of each.

There are several variations or types of statements that can be used to summarize the changes of the rights of owners (e.g., statement of retained earnings, statement of surplus, statement of changes in net worth, statement of shareholders' equity, etc.). The type your business uses will depend on the nature of your business, and your accountant's preference. However, the purpose of all of these "changes" statements is :

1. The amounts of the owners' rights at the beginning of the period.
2. The increases or decreases during that period.
3. The amount of rights at the end of the period.

Statements of owners' equity for a corporation: A corporate owners' (stockholders') equity statement shows the paid-in capital invested in the business in exchange for stock, as of the beginning of the accounting period. It also shows how the income shown on the Income Statement was paid out as dividends, or plowed back into the business as retained earnings.

The creation of your financial statements is largely a mechanical exercise. The numbers to be used are found in your accounting records after the books are closed at the end of the period; to draw up the statements, you, your accountant, or your accounting software simply look up the numbers and plug them into the statement.

Using the numbers to your benefit:The real value to the statements comes after their creation, when you analyze them to see how your business is doing in numerous areas. You don't have to know the exact makeup of each item on the balance sheet and income statement, but you must have a sense of what the numbers mean in order to interpret and analyze these financial records. Raw data in isolation does not make sense — it is in relation to what that counts.

5

BASIC OF BOOKKEEPING

As a small business owner, you probably rely on an outside accountant to do your taxes and prepare financial statements. However, like many small business owners, you may find that it's too expensive to pay an accountant to do routine bookkeeping chores. Someone in your organisation must take on the responsibility of keeping an accurate set of financial records. Fortunately, you may find this task easier than you thought, especially if you use your computer.

5.1. IMPORTANCE OF GOOD RECORDS

Unless your business is accounting or bookkeeping, keeping financial records is probably not what you do best. Most likely, you'd rather spend your time selling your product or service. However, if you are going to run a successful business, accurate and timely financial information is a must. Here are some of the reasons why you need a good financial recordkeeping system:

Monitoring the success or failure of your business: It's hard to know how your business is doing without a clear financial picture. Am I making money? Are sales increasing? Are expenditures increasing faster than sales? Which expenses are too high based on my level of sales? Do some expenditures appear to be "out of control?"

Providing the information you need to make decisions: Evaluating the financial consequences should be a part of every business decision you make. Without accurate records and financial information, it may be hard for you to know the financial impact of a given course of action. Will it pay to hire another salesperson? How much will another production employee cost? Is this particular product line profitable?

Obtaining bank financing: A banker will usually want to see financial statements: a balance sheet, income statement, and cash flow budget for the most current and prior years, as well as your projected statements showing the impact of the requested loan. A banker may even want to see some of your bookkeeping procedures and documents to verify whether you run your business in a sound, professional manner.

Obtaining other sources of capital: If your business has reached the point where you need to take in a partner, any prospective partner will want to become intimately familiar with your financial picture. If you need capital and are thinking of taking in an outside investor, you will need to produce a lot of financial information. Even your suppliers and other creditors may ask to see certain financial records. Such information may be produced by your outside accountant, but it is based on your day-to-day record keeping.

Budgeting: All businesses should use a budget for planning purposes. A budget will help keep your business on track by forecasting your cash needs and helping you control expenditures. In addition, if you are seeking bank financing or other sources of capital, a banker or prospective investor will probably want to see your budget as evidence that your business is well planned and stable. You must have solid financial information to prepare a meaningful budget.

Preparing your income tax return: Whether your business is a sole proprietorship, partnership, or corporation, you must file an income tax return and pay income taxes. With good records, preparing an accurate tax return will be easier and you're more likely to be able to do it on time. Poor records may result in your underpaying or overpaying your taxes and/or filing late (and paying penalties).

If your accountant prepares your income tax return, poor records will almost certainly result in your paying higher accounting fees. If your business is a partnership, not only will you have to prepare a partnership tax return, but partnership return amounts will pass directly to the tax return of each partner. So your recordkeeping will directly affect the tax return of each partner.

Complying with federal and state payroll tax rules: If you have employees, you are aware of the myriad rules and regulations relating to payroll taxes. Payroll tax deposits must be made according to strict deadlines. Late payment of payroll taxes results in severe, and unnecessary, penalties. Also, you must file a payroll tax return every quarter, which you must reconcile with the payroll deposits made during the quarter.

Then at the end of the year, you are required to give your employees and the government W-2 forms, which must agree with your quarterly payroll returns. Sound bookkeeping practices will make compliance with all these payroll rules easy. Poor records will make it impossible.

Submitting sales taxes: If you collect sales tax from your customers, good records will make it easy for you to compute the tax due and prepare the required reports.

Distributing profits: If your business is a partnership, you will need good records to determine the correct amount of profits to distribute to each partner. If you are operating as a corporation, you must determine the company profits that you will be paying out as dividends to the shareholders.

5.2. WORKING WITH YOUR ACCOUNTANT

In most cases, with a little study and help from computer software tools, you should be able to manage your most basic financial records without the help of an accountant. This includes the daily recording of transactions, maintenance of a general ledger, and maintenance of your cash records. There are some other records you may need to maintain, depending on your business, such as accounts receivable ledgers and accounts payable ledgers.

You may need an accountant to help with less routine tasks, such as preparing periodic adjusting entries, financial statements, closing entries, and income tax returns, or helping you prepare a budget. You may also decide to have your accountant set up your books when you first open your business. If you've been in business for a while, your accountant could give your bookkeeping procedures and records a one-time or periodic checkup.

At a minimum, you will need your accountant to help you close the books annually because you have to file an income tax return every year. If you are having financial statements prepared, you will want them done at least annually. However, annual financial statements may not be enough to help you keep tabs on your business. You may want financial statements every quarter, or even monthly. Depending on the size of your business, you may want to have your accountant close the books every month, particularly if you need to submit monthly sales tax to the state.

1. Selecting an accountant.
2. Getting records ready for the accountant.

5.3. ACCOUNTING SYSTEM

Before you can set up your accounting records, dive into your day-to-day transactions, and get your books ready for end-of-month or end-of-year reporting, you must gain an understanding of basic accounting concepts.

Accounting is the method in which financial information is gathered, processed, and summarised into financial statements and reports. An accounting system can be represented by the following graphic, which is explained below. Every accounting entry is based on a business transaction, which is usually evidenced by a business document, such as a check or a sales invoice.

A journal is a place to record the transactions of a business. The typical journals used to record the chronological, day-to-day transactions are sales and cash receipts journals and a cash disbursements journal. A general journal is used to record special entries at the end of an accounting period.

While a journal records transactions as they happen, a ledger groups transactions according to their type, based on the accounts they affect. The general ledger is a collection of all balance sheet, income, and expense accounts used to keep a business's accounting records. At the end of an accounting period, all journal entries are summarised and transferred to the general ledger accounts. This procedure is called "posting."

A trial balance is prepared at the end of an accounting period by adding up all the account balances in your general ledger. The sum of the debit balances should equal the sum of the credit balances. If total debits don't equal total credits, you must track down the errors.

Finally, financial statements are prepared from the information in your trial balance. Your accounting records are important because the resulting financial statements and reports help you plan and make decisions.

They may be used by some third parties (bankers, investors, or creditors) and are needed to provide information to government agencies, such as the Internal Revenue Service.

5.3.1. Daily Recording of Transactions

In order to take control of your financial recordkeeping, you must accurately record your day-to-day sales, purchases, and other transactions. Specifically, you need to record:

1. Sales and revenue transactions.
2. Cash transactions.
3. Accounts receivable, if you extend credit to your customers.
4. Accounts payable, if you purchase from your suppliers on credit.
5. Summaries of transactions in your general ledger.

If possible, you may want to keep a separate set of books for each. Separate accounting will provide you with more meaningful information. It may show you that one product line or department is profitable, and another is not. Unfortunately, it may be difficult to keep a separate set of books for each product line or department. For example, some or all expenses may not apply to only one department, but must be allocated among departments. You should seek the advice of an accountant before setting up an accounting system of this nature.

There are many computer programs on the market to help you automate your accounting procedures. Shop around. Accounting software is sold in office supply stores, software outlets, electronics stores, mail order houses, and directly from software publishers. Ask for your accountant's opinion. Your accountant may want you to use a program that is compatible with the system he or she uses.

If you have employees, look for accounting software that permits the use of passwords to control access to all or some of your accounting transactions. In order to prevent irregularities by your employees or others, it's wise to restrict access to your accounting records.

Whether your business is a sole proprietorship, partnership, or corporation, always keep your personal transactions separate from your business transactions. For example, using business funds to pay for personal expenditures complicates your recordkeeping and can lead to serious tax problems. It can also result in some hefty accounting fees as you pay your accountant to sort it all out.

5.4. REVENUE TRANSACTIONS

You record daily sales in a sales journal. To simplify your bookkeeping, a combined sales and cash receipts journal. With a journal that combines sales and cash receipts, you record all sales (cash and credit) and all cash receipts, including collection of accounts receivable, in one journal. Entries in your sales and cash receipts journal come from the source documents you use in your business every day. These documents are sales invoices, daily cash register totals, daily cash sheets, and daily sales registers.

Sales invoices: If you use sales invoices, you will post the information from each invoice to an entry in the sales journal. If you maintain customer charge accounts, you will also be posting entries to the accounts receivable ledgers so that each customer account is up-to-date. Sales invoices should be numbered. At a minimum, prepare two copies; give one copy to the customer, and retain the other. Preferably, you should prepare the invoices in triplicate, with two copies retained by you.

File one by customer name; the other by invoice number. Include canceled or voided invoices when filing by number, so that you can account for all of them. The invoice should show the date of the sale, quantity, if applicable, price or rate, an extension column, if applicable (quantity multiplied by price), and a payment due date. If you use a computer software program to perform your accounting, it probably has a pre-designed sales invoice that you can use.

Cash register totals: If you use a cash register, daily sales can be totaled on the register. Most new cash registers should be able to separately record cash sales and charge sales, and keep track of sales tax. Some should also be able to record cash received on account. At the end of the business day, record your cash register totals in the sales journal.

Cash sheets and sales registers: If you don't use a cash register, you can record cash receipts on a daily cash sheet and record sales on a columnar sales register. The sales register is simply a record of each sale for the day. Total the cash sheet and sales register at the end of the day. Enter the totals in the sales and cash receipts journal.

5.4.1. Cash Receipts Journal

There are many different types of sales journals and cash receipts journals available. To simplify your bookkeeping, a combined sales and cash receipts journal. If you are going to be recording sales and cash receipts manually in a journal, visit an office supply store. They will have many different kinds for you to choose from. Look at the different column headings, and choose the one that best meets the needs of your business. If you will be using computer software, you probably won't have to decide which type of journal to use.

Your program will probably have some type of sales and cash receipts journal, but may allow you to customize it based on your type of business. If the sum of the debit columns doesn't equal the sum of the credit columns, you have a problem that you should investigate right away. You may have recorded one of the amounts in the wrong column. Maybe you charged the customer the wrong amount. Or you might have simply added incorrectly when computing the totals. It is usually easy to pinpoint the error because the debits should equal the credits for each transaction.

Your sales and cash receipts journal will probably have more columns than our sample. For example, you could have more than one column for "Sales" by splitting your sales into categories. You might have one column labelled "Parts and Supplies Sales" and another labelled "Service and Repair Revenue." This could provide you with more meaningful information. The way you do business might require additional columns. For example, if you give a discount to your charge customers who pay within 10 days, you could add a column labelled "Sales Discounts Dr."

5.5. CASH TRANSACTIONS

A typical small business has a variety of different types of cash transactions, which should be recorded in a number of different places:

Sales and cash receipts journal: to simplify your recordkeeping, you combine your sales and cash receipts in a combined journal.

Daily cash sheet: if a lot of cash moves in and out of your business each day, you should also prepare a daily cash sheet to reconcile your cash received and paid out for the day. If you use a daily cash sheet, you can reconcile your cash receipts with your daily deposit into your bank account.

A bank reconciliation: a bank reconciliation, at the end of every month, verifies the amount you have in your checking account. It will also help you find bookkeeping errors and could help prevent irregularities such as employee theft.

A cash disbursements journal: your daily cash disbursements should be recorded here.

A petty cash fund: if your customers normally pay by check, you may need to set up so that you will have some currency on hand to pay miscellaneous small expenses. A petty cash fund isn't necessary if you use a cash register and always have currency on hand, as long you keep track of these small purchases.

5.5.1. Daily Cash Sheets

A cash sheet is a daily reconciliation of cash received and cash paid out. If a lot of your business is transacted in cash, such as in a retail store, you should prepare a cash sheet at the end of each day. Deposit all cash receipts in your bank account daily. Your daily cash receipts should generally be the same amount as your daily bank deposit. If they are not the same, you should investigate and reconcile the two amounts. Any reasons for a difference should be apparent on your cash sheet, such as a small amount of cash paid out for a miscellaneous expense.

An important reason to do a cash sheet is to alert you to any shortage or surplus of cash for the day. Some businesses that do not prepare a cash sheet simply count the cash in the register at the end of the day. Without doing a reconciliation, they don't discover any shortages or overages. A shortage could be the result of theft, or it could simply result from your failure to record a special transaction, such as an expense you paid in cash.

5.5.2. Bank Reconciliation

Prepare a bank reconciliation when you receive your bank statement every month. This is a very important part of your cash control procedures. It verifies the amount of cash you have in your checking account. The cash balance in your books will never agree with the balance shown on the bank statement because of the delay in checks and deposits clearing the bank, automatic bank charges and credits you haven't recorded, and errors you may have made in your books.

After preparing the bank reconciliation, you can be comfortable that the account balance shown on your books is up-to-date. Another important reason to do a bank reconciliation is that it may uncover irregularities such as employee theft of funds. Here are step-by-step instructions for preparing a bank reconciliation.

Prepare a list of deposits in transit: Compare the deposits listed on your bank statement with the bank deposits shown in your cash receipts journal. On your bank reconciliation, list any deposits that have not yet cleared the bank statement. Also, take a look at the bank reconciliation you prepared last month.

Prepare a list of outstanding checks: In your cash disbursements journal, mark each check that cleared the bank statement this month. On your bank reconciliation, list all the checks from the cash disbursements journal that did not clear. Also, take a look at the bank reconciliation you prepared last month.

Are there any checks that were outstanding last month that still have not cleared the bank? If so, be sure they are on your list of outstanding checks this month. If a check is several months old and still has not cleared the bank, you may want to investigate further.

Record any bank charges or credits: Take a close look at your bank statement. Are there any special charges made by the bank that you have not recorded in your books? If so, record them now just as you would have if you had written a check for that amount. By the same token, if there are any credits made to your account by the bank, those should be recorded as well. Post the entries to your general ledger.

Compute the cash balance per your books: Foot the general ledger cash account to arrive at your ending cash balance.

Enter bank balance on the reconciliation: At the top of the bank reconciliation, enter the ending balance from the bank statement.

Total the deposits in transit: Add up the deposits in transit, and enter the total on the reconciliation. Add the total deposits in transit to the bank balance to arrive at a subtotal.

Total the outstanding checks: Add up the outstanding checks, and enter the total on the reconciliation.

Compute book balance per the reconciliation: Subtract the total outstanding checks from the subtotal in step 6 above. The result should equal the balance shown in your general ledger.

If your bank reconciliation doesn't balance, you need to find the error or errors. Here are the possible causes of a bank balance error:

1. Total outstanding checks added incorrectly: Double check your addition of the total outstanding checks.
2. Total deposits in transit added incorrectly. Double check your addition of deposits in transit.
3. Bank balance written down incorrectly. Did you start with the correct amount at the top of your reconciliation? Double check by comparing it to the month end balance on your bank statement.

4. Failed to record all items clearing the bank statement. Look at your bank statement carefully. Are there any items, such as miscellaneous bank charges or automatic deposits or withdrawals, that were not recorded in your books?
5. Journals added incorrectly. Double check your addition of cash receipts and cash disbursements.
6. Failed to record a check or deposit. Did you record all checks and deposits in your journals? This should have been apparent when you were preparing your lists of deposits in transit and outstanding checks.
7. Incorrectly recorded an amount. Compare each item on the bank statement with your journal entry for that item. Did you enter the correct amount?

5.5.3. Cash Disbursements Journal

A cash disbursements journal is where you record your cash (or check) paid-out transactions. It can also be called a purchases journal or an expense journal. There are many different types and styles of cash disbursements journals. If you will be recording expenses manually in a journal, visit an office supply store.

They should have different types to choose from. Look at the column headings, and choose the journal that best meets the needs of your business. You might consider a disbursements journal that is integrated with your checkbook — this may save you some time because your journal entry is made at the same time as you write the check.

If you are using computer software, you probably won't have to decide which type of journal to use. Your program will probably have some type of disbursements journal, but may allow you to customize it based on your business needs. If you use the accrual basis of accounting, you'll record expenses at the time you purchase goods or services, even if you purchase on credit.

If the sum of the debit columns doesn't equal the sum of the credit columns, you have a problem that you should track down right away. You may have entered one of the amounts in the wrong column. You might have simply added incorrectly when computing the totals. It is usually easy to pinpoint the error because the debits should equal the credits for each transaction. Your purchases journal may have many more columns than this sample because you probably will have more expense classifications.

5.5.4. Petty Cash Fund

Set up a petty cash fund if you need cash on hand to pay miscellaneous small expenses of your business. If yours is a retail business with cash on hand, you probably don't need a petty cash fund. Just be sure to carefully record all cash paid out of the cash register. Preparing a cash sheet at the end of the day will help control cash paid out of the register.

A petty cash fund is set up and used as follows:

1. Start a petty cash fund by writing a check to "Petty Cash." Cash the check.
2. Physically place the cash in a petty cash drawer or petty cash box.
3. As you pay for expenses out of petty cash, keep an itemised list of each expenditure.
4. When the cash is almost depleted, add up the expenses on your itemised list.
5. Write another check to "Petty Cash" for the total of the expenses. That check should replenish the fund back to the initial balance.

6. The petty cash drawer or box should be locked when not in use. Only one person should have access to the petty cash, so that one person is held accountable for it.

5.5.5. Accounts Receivable

Accounts receivable are unpaid customer invoices, and any other money owed to you by your customers. The sum of all your customer accounts receivable is listed as a current asset on your balance sheet. You should keep an accounts receivable ledger account for each customer. The accounts receivable ledger, which can also double as a customer statement, is a record of each customer's charges and payments.

When a customer purchases something, you'll first record the sale in the sales and cash receipts journal. This journal will have accounts receivable debit and credit columns. Charge sales and payments on account are entered in these two columns, respectively. Then, each day, the credit sales recorded in the sales and cash receipts journal is posted to the appropriate customer's accounts in the accounts receivable ledger. This allows you to know not only the total amount owed to you by all credit customers, but also the total amount owed by each customer.

Entries made in the sales and cash receipts journal are also totaled at the end of the month, and the results are posted to the accounts receivable account in your general ledger. This account is your accounts receivable "control account." What "control" means is that after all your posting is completed, the total amount of customer balances in the accounts receivable ledger will be the same as the balance in the control account in the general ledger. If they aren't the same, you can tell that you made an error somewhere along the line.

If you extend credit to your customers and maintain a sales and cash receipts journal by hand, look for a journal that integrates posting to the accounts receivable ledgers with the recording of sales and cash receipts transactions. This is called a "one-write" system. It will usually save you time and cut down on posting errors. If you use a computer program, posting to the accounts receivable ledgers will occur automatically.

Accounts receivable ledger: You must maintain an accounts receivable ledger account for each customer you extend credit to. Post your sales invoice charges from the sales and cash receipts journal to the customer ledgers at the end of each day. Also, whether you use a cash register or a separate cash receipts book, be sure to post cash receipts on account to the appropriate ledgers at the end of the day.

Keep all your accounts receivable ledgers in one binder: To save paperwork, copies of the accounts receivable ledgers also serve as the statements you mail to your customers in request for payment. If you are going to mail them out as statements, begin a new ledger sheet every month. The monthly ledger sheet should start with a balance forward, which is the ending balance from the previous month.

If your ledger sheets will not be doubling as your customer statements, you don't need to start a new sheet every month. Just keep a permanent ledger for each customer that maintains a running total of the customer balance. For most businesses, statements should be sent once a month to all customers with an account balance. The statement should show the following:

1. A beginning balance (the previous month's ending balance).
2. All invoices charged during the month.
3. Payments on account during the month.

4. Any debit memos or credit memos.
5. An ending balance.
6. A due date.

When you mail statements to your customers every month, you should reconcile your accounts receivable ledgers with the accounts receivable control account. The control account is the total accounts receivable balance from your general ledger. The beginning accounts receivable total, plus charge sales for the month, minus payments on account for the month, should equal the ending accounts receivable total. Compare this amount to the sum of the individual customer accounts receivable ledgers. This will help you discover any errors in your customer statements before you mail them out. This is a valuable cash management tool which you will use to contact past due customers.

5.5.6. Accounts Payable

Accounts payable are the unpaid bills of the business; the money you owe to your suppliers and other creditors. The sum of the amounts you owe to your suppliers is listed as a current liability on your balance sheet. If you use the accrual basis of accounting, expenses are recorded in the cash disbursements journal at the time the goods or services are purchased, even if you buy on credit. If you deal with a given supplier many times during the month, you don't have to record every purchase.

You could accumulate all bills for the month from that supplier, then record one transaction in the purchases journal at the end of the month. You should keep an accounts payable ledger account for each supplier. Expenses from the cash disbursements journal are, at the end of each day, posted to the appropriate accounts payable ledger. The accounts payable ledger is a record of what you owe each vendor.

The general ledger contains an accounts payable account, which is your accounts payable control account. The cash disbursements journal has accounts payable credit and debit columns. Credit purchases and payments on account are entered in these two columns, respectively. At the end of the month they are totaled and posted to the control account in the general ledger.

Accounts payable ledgers: Accounts payable ledgers will help you control your expenditures and payables. If you maintain accurate payable ledgers, it will be easy for you to double check the bills you get from your suppliers. At the end of the month, reconcile your accounts payable ledgers with the accounts payable control account. The control account is the total accounts payable balance from your general ledger.

The beginning accounts payable total, plus purchases on account during the month, minus payments on account during the month, should equal the ending accounts payable total. Compare this amount to the sum of the individual accounts payable ledgers. This will help you discover any errors you made in recording your payables. A reconciliation might also help you catch any errors on vendor bills. An accounts payable aging report is a good cash management tool that should be prepared periodically. It will help you plan the timing and amount of your cash disbursements.

5.5.7. General Ledger

The general ledger is a permanent summary of all your supporting journals, such as the sales and cash receipts journal and the cash disbursements journal. Your financial statements are built from the general ledger.

For each account title shown on your sales and cash receipts journal columns and your cash disbursements journal columns, there is a general ledger account. There are also separate general ledger accounts for miscellaneous items that don't have their own column in the journals, but are entered in a "miscellaneous" column.

For example, Cash, Accounts receivable, Accounts payable, Sales, Purchases, Telephone expense, and Owners equity are all examples of general ledger accounts. There is a page reserved in the general ledger for each general ledger account.

The individual entries in the general ledger are always from the total columns of your supporting journals. When all journal entries are posted, you can arrive at the ending balance for each account. The sum of all general ledger debit balances should always equal the sum of all general ledger credit balances.

5.6. CLOSING THE BOOKS

When you reach the end of an accounting period, you need to "close the books." At a minimum, you will close your books annually because you have to file an income tax return every year. If you are having financial statements prepared, you will want them done at least annually. However, annual financial statements may not be enough to help you keep tabs on your business. You may want financial statements monthly, bimonthly, or quarterly.

Even if you are not having financial statements prepared, you may want to close your books monthly. Sending out customer statements, paying your suppliers, reconciling your bank statement, and submitting sales tax reports to the state are probably some of the tasks you need to do every month. You may find it easier to do these if you close your books.

1. *How to close your books*: After you finish entering the day-to-day transactions in your journals, you are ready to "close the books" for the period. A step-

by-step description of how to close the books follows. How many of the steps you do yourself depends on how much of the accounting you want to do, and how much you want to pay your accountant to do.

2. *Post entries to the general ledger*: Transfer the account totals from your journals (sales and cash receipts journal and cash disbursements journal) to your general ledger accounts.
3. *Total the general ledger accounts*: By footing the general ledger accounts, you will arrive at a preliminary ending balance for each account.
4. *Prepare a preliminary trial balance*: Add all of the general ledger account ending balances together. Total debits should equal total credits. This will help assure you that your accounts balance prior to making adjusting entries.
5. *Prepare adjusting journal entries*: Certain end-of-period adjustments must be made before you can close your books. Adjusting entries are required to account for items that don't get recorded in your daily transactions. In a traditional accounting system, adjusting entries are made in a general journal.
6. *Foot the general ledger accounts again*: This will give you the adjusted balance of each general ledger account.
7. *Prepare an adjusted trial balance*: Prepare another trial balance, using the adjusted balances of each general ledger account. Again, total debits must equal total credits.
8. *Prepare financial statements*: After tracking down and correcting any trial balance errors, you (or your accountant) are ready to prepare a balance sheet and income statement.

9. *Prepare closing entries*: Get your general ledger ready for the next accounting period by clearing out the revenue and expense accounts and transferring the net income or loss to owner's equity. This is done by preparing journal entries that are called closing entries in a general journal.
10. *Prepare a post-closing trial balance*: After you make closing entries, all revenue and expense accounts will have a zero balance. Prepare one more trial balance. Since all revenue and expense accounts have been closed out to zero, this trial balance will only contain balance sheet accounts. Remember that the total debit balance must equal the total credit balance. This will help ensure that all general ledger account balances are correct as of the beginning of the new accounting period.

5.6.1. Trial Balance

The trial balance is a worksheet on which you list all your general ledger accounts and their debit or credit balance. It is a tool that is used to alert you to errors in your books. The total debits must equal the total credits. If they don't equal, you know you have an error that must be tracked down.

When closing out your books at the end of an accounting period, you will prepare three trial balances:

1. A preliminary trial balance is prepared using your general ledger account balances before you make adjusting entries.
2. An adjusted trial balance is done after preparing adjusting entries and posting them to your general ledger. This will help ensure that the books used to prepare your financial statements are in balance.

3. A post-closing trial balance is done after preparing and posting your closing entries. This trial balance, which should contain only balance sheet accounts, will help guarantee that your books are in balance for the beginning of the new accounting period.

In other words, what if total debits don't equal total credits? This shouldn't surprise or discourage you. In fact, it might be more surprising if it does balance. Accounting errors happen. Even experienced bookkeepers normally have to find trial balance errors.

5.6.2. General Journal

The general journal is usually a two-column journal used for unusual and annual accounting entries that aren't recorded in the sales and cash receipts and cash disbursements journals. Adjusting entries and closing entries, made at the end of an accounting period, are the most common entries made in the general journal. The general journal is also used to record special transactions that don't get recorded in one of the regular journals General journal entries are posted to the respective general ledger accounts.

5.6.3. Adjusting Entries

Certain end-of-period adjustments must be made when you close your books. Adjusting entries are made at the end of an accounting period to account for items that don't get recorded in your daily transactions. In a traditional accounting system, adjusting entries are made in a general journal.

Some adjusting entries are straightforward. Others require judgment and some accounting knowledge. You will have to decide if you are going to tackle some or all adjusting entries, or if you want to pay your accountant to do them. If your accountant prepares adjusting entries, he or she should give you a copy of these entries so that you can enter them in your general ledger.

5.7. PREPARING FINANCIAL STATEMENTS

After you have prepared your adjusting entries in the general journal, posted the general journal totals to the general ledger, and footed the general ledger accounts, you are ready to prepare financial statements. If all adjusting entries have been made, and a trial balance done, preparing financial statements is really just a matter of putting the trial balance amounts onto properly formatted statements.

The financial statements prepared for most small businesses are:

1. a balance sheet
2. an income statement

Usually these are prepared by an accountant. But with the help of computer software, you may be able to prepare your own financial statements. If you need to prepare financial statements for third parties, such as a banker, sometimes the third party may request that the financial statements be prepared by a professional accountant or certified public accountant.

5.7.1. Balance Sheet

Also called a statement of financial position, a balance sheet is a financial "snapshot" of your business at a given date in time. It lists your assets, your liabilities, and the difference between the two, which is your owner's equity, or net worth. The accounting equation (assets = liabilities + owner's equity) is the basis for the balance sheet.

The balance sheet is prepared after all adjusting entries are made in the general journal, all journal entries have been posted to the general ledger, the general ledger accounts have been footed to arrive at the period end totals, and an adjusted trial balance is prepared from the general ledger amounts. Financial statements normally do not show cents. All amounts should be rounded to the nearest dollar.

5.8. INCOME STATEMENT

Also called a profit and loss statement, or a "P&L," an income statement lists your income, expenses, and net income (or loss). The net income (or loss) is equal to your income minus your expenses. Your business's tax return will use a variation of the income statement to determine your potentially taxable income.

The income statement is prepared after all adjusting entries are made in the general journal, all journal entries have been posted to the general ledger, the general ledger accounts have been footed to arrive at the period end totals, and an adjusted trial balance has been prepared from the general ledger totals. Financial statements normally do not show cents. All amounts should be rounded to the nearest dollar.

5.8.1. Closing Entries

After financial statements are prepared, you are ready to get your books ready for the next accounting period by clearing out the income and expense accounts in the general ledger and transferring the net income (or loss) to your owner's equity account. This is done by preparing closing entries in the general journal.

Note the distinction between adjusting entries and closing entries. Adjusting entries are required to update certain accounts in your general ledger at the end of an accounting period. They must be done before you can prepare your financial statements and income tax return. Closing entries are needed to clear out your revenue and expense accounts as you start the beginning of a new accounting period. Preparing your closing entries is a very simple, mechanical process. Follow these steps:

1. Close the revenue accounts. Prepare one journal entry that debits all the revenue accounts. (These accounts will have a credit balance in the general ledger prior to the closing entry.) Credit an account called "income summary" for the total.
2. Close the expense accounts. Prepare one journal entry that credits all the expense accounts. (These accounts will have a debit balance in the general ledger prior to the closing entry.) Debit the income summary account for the total.
3. Transfer the income summary balance to a capital account. Prepare a journal entry that clears out the income summary account. This entry effectively transfers the net income (or loss) of the business to the owner's equity account.
4. Close the drawing account. If your business is a sole proprietorship or partnership, close the drawing accounts (if any) by preparing a journal entry that credits the drawing account and debits the owner's equity account.

After all closing entries are made, post the entry totals to the general ledger. Foot the general ledger accounts to arrive at the beginning amounts for the new accounting period. All revenue and expense accounts should have a zero balance.

6

GETTING THE MONEY TO EMPLOYEES

Automatic deposit of employees' wages directly into their bank accounts can streamline payroll operations, increase productivity, and save money for your business. A direct deposit transaction can cost as little as four or five cents to process, versus 30 to 50 cents for a check. In a direct deposit program, employee pay is deposited right into the employees' personal accounts, eliminating costly steps in the payroll process, including the need to stop payment on and reissue lost or stolen checks.

Direct deposit means fewer check processing charges and reconcilement maintenance fees from the employer's financial institution. First, determine what the state laws are where you employ individuals. Most states require that direct deposit be voluntary and prohibit you from barring individual employees from participating in direct deposit programs. Some also require that you provide a statement of wages so employees can see what was deposited in their accounts and what deductions were made.

You may set up a direct deposit relationship with a bank of your choice or the employee's choice. Call those institutions that you are interested in dealing with and have them spend some time telling you about their program. Some may require a certain number of participants and some may require that you have electronic capability with the Automated Clearing House (ACH). When you communicate your direct deposit program to your employees, be sure to highlight the benefits of direct deposit for them and have a form available for employees to elect direct deposit or to modify their choice.

6.1. INFORMATION TO PROVIDE WITH PAY

If your employees are paid by check or participate in a direct deposit program, you should provide them with a statement that details their gross wages, what deductions have been made, and what their net pay is. In fact, some states require that a statement of some sort be provided to employees when they are paid.

6.1.1. Rules to Distributing Pay

To be on the safe side, there are a number of rules that you should follow when you are distributing pay:

1. Deliver pay to each employee personally and discreetly.
2. Encourage employees not to leave checks or money in an unsecured area.
3. Do not leave one employee's pay with another employee (unless it's a supervisor) to be delivered.
4. Do not allow relatives of the employee to pick up an employee's pay if the employee is out on sick leave or vacation unless you have express permission from the employee.
5. If you have a regularly scheduled pay period, such as every two weeks, try to distribute the pay at the same time of day on payday, so employees know when to expect their pay.

6. If you pay employees with checks, in the interest of confidentiality, you might want to put the checks in individual envelopes.
7. If you have to mail an employee's check because the employee is out on sick leave or vacation, use certified, insured mail.
8. Never demean employees or require them to perform tasks or make statements to get their checks, even if you're just joking with them.

6.1.2. Employment Terminates

When employment terminates, there are certain things you'll have to take care of, including issuing the employee's last pay check. If possible, it's best to give the check to the employee on the last day of employment. In some cases (for instance, when you fire an employee), you may not have enough time to prepare the pay check before the employee leaves. In that event, you should get the check to the employee as soon as possible.

7

HOW TO SAVE MY MONEY

Saving is simply a way to use your current income for something in the future. You can save for a variety of reasons: for purchasing a new television in a couple of months, a new car, college expenses, the down payment on a car or a house, or to support yourself during retirement. Just as there are many reasons to save, there are also many ways to save. In many cases, the best way to save depends on your future plans.

7.1. FACTORS TO SAVE

Ask yourself these questions:

1. How accessible do I want my money to be?
2. How much interest will I earn?
3. Is there any possibility that I will lose my money?

The first question most directly relates to the reason for saving. If you are saving for a short period of time or for an emergency, you may want an account that will give you easy access to your money, such as a passbook savings account or a money market account.

Keeping money in a checking account is another way to "save" for a short time. You can get money quickly, but at an additional cost. Sometimes, when the goal is years away, it is better to save your money in a way that you will not be tempted to use it for other things. Choosing the right bank, savings and loan or credit union is an important decision. These institutions may have different types of accounts, fees and hours of operation.

A small bank in your neighbourhood may give you more personal service. A large bank with offices in grocery stores or with many ATM machines is convenient. Credit unions may loan funds at slightly lower interest rates. Another consideration is whether your account is protected by deposit insurance. If you want to earn a higher interest rate, you may choose a certificate of deposit (CD).

With a CD, your money is in the account for a specified length of time. Usually, the longer the time, the higher the interest rate. Maturity terms for CDs can range from a couple of months to periods of several years. If, for some reason, you want the money from your CD prior to the set time, you will give up some of the interest you may have earned. Even more gain is possible if you invest in stocks, mutual funds or bonds. You may earn more, but there is the risk that you will lose some or all of your money.

If you want to be sure you will always have your money, an insured account is important. Risky investments can pay much higher dividends, but with a greater possibility that you might lose money. Traditionally, savings that are safe and gain a guaranteed rate of interest are referred to as just "savings." Methods that are riskier and that may gain or lose more are called "investments." Some combination of traditional savings and investments may be a good savings plan. The key is deciding why you are saving and how much you can afford to save.

7.2. REASONS TO SAVE

1. For short-term saving — a night out next Friday—maybe dropping a few dollar and change in a jar each day will work.
2. For long-term goals — a home purchase or college—putting your money somewhere it will be safe and grow is important.
3. For emergencies—a new water heater or an unexpected bill—you may want quick access to your savings.
4. For large planned purchases—a new car or a vacation—you may want to keep it in a place where you will not be tempted to spend it.
5. For your retirement, you will want to save in a way that is absolutely safe and gives the best long-term return for your deposits.

7.2.1. Saving Early

There are advantages to saving early in life. Your benefit from savings is a function of two things: the amount you save and the interest rate or return that you receive. When interest compounds, interest is paid on interest.

Example of Compound Interest: Mary put Rs. 50,000 in a savings account at 5% interest. After one year, the account balance was Rs. 52,500. Rs. 2,500 interest was paid to her account. After another year, her balance was Rs. 55,125. In the second year, her interest was Rs. 2,500 on the original Rs. 50,000 and another Rs. 125 interest on the Rs. 2,500 interest from the first year. In the next year, she will earn 5% interest on Rs. 55,125.

One sure thing is that the earlier you start saving, the more you will accumulate over time.

7.2.2. Costs and Benefits of Saving

1. *Risk*: Some savings methods are very safe. Saving accounts in banks are insured by an agency of the federal government. The chances of losing your savings are very small. On the other hand, shares of stock may rapidly gain or lose value.
2. *Return*: Some savings methods pay interest or dividends, thus, increasing the value of the savings. Stock purchases may greatly increase in value over the years. Bonds will pay a set interest rate. The interest paid on municipal bonds is usually tax-free. Your real gain increases by the amount of the tax savings.
3. *Liquidity*: Some types of saving allow you quick access to your money. Others make it more difficult. A bank savings account can be accessed whenever the bank is open or through using an ATM. Stocks and bonds are sometimes difficult to sell unless you are willing to take a loss.

7.3. BEFORE SPENT MONEY

For most kinds of purchases, you can get valuable advice and comparisons on the Internet. Ask a librarian or friends which Internet sites they think are helpful, or you can use a search engine like Google or Yahoo. Be aware that information you find is often biased. At many websites, the only products or sellers listed are ones that pay to advertise. Before buying anything on the Internet, check several websites and make sure you deal with reputable dealers.

7.3.1. Transportation

Airline Fares: Compare low-cost carriers with major carriers that fly to your destination. Remember, the best fares may not be out of the airport closest to you. You may save by including a Saturday evening stay-over or by purchasing the ticket at least 14 days in advance. Ask which days of the week and times of the day have the lowest fare. Even if you are using a travel agent, check airline and internet travel sites, and look for special deals. If you call, always ask for the lowest fare to your destination.

Car Rental: Since car rental rates can vary greatly, compare total price (including taxes and surcharge) and take advantage of any special offers and membership discounts. Rental car companies offer various insurance and waiver options. Check with your automobile insurance agent and credit card company in advance to avoid duplicating any coverage you may already have.

New Cars: You can save thousands of dollars over the lifetime of a car by selecting a model that combines a low purchase price with low depreciation, financing, insurance, gasoline, maintenance, and repair costs. Ask your local librarian for new car guides that contain this information.

Having selected a model and options you are interested in, you can save hundreds of dollars by comparison shopping. Get price quotes from several dealers (over the phone or internet) and let each know you are contacting the others.

Used Cars: Before buying any used car: Compare the seller's asking price with the average retail price in a "bluebook" or other guide to car prices which can be found at many libraries, banks, and credit unions. Have a mechanic you trust check the car, especially if the car is sold "as is."

Consider purchasing a used car from an individual you know and trust. They are more likely than other sellers to charge a lower price and point out any problems with the car.

Auto Leasing: Don't decide to lease a car just because the payments are lower than on a traditional auto loan. The leasing payments are lower because you don't actually own the car. Leasing a car is very complicated. When shopping, consider the price of the car (known as the capitalised cost), your trade-in allowance, any down payment, monthly payments, various fees (excess mileage, excess "wear and tear," end-of- lease), and the cost of buying the car at the end of the lease. A valuable source of information about auto leasing can be found in Keys to Vehicle Leasing: A Consumer Guide, which is published by the Federal Reserve Board and Federal Trade Commission.

Gasoline: You can save hundreds of dollars a year by comparing prices at different stations, pumping gas yourself, and using the lowest-octane called for in your owner's manual. You can save up to Rs. 5,000 a year on gas by keeping your engine tuned and your tires inflated to their proper pressure.

Car Repairs: Consumers lose billions of dollars each year on unneeded or poorly done car repairs. The most important step that you can take to save money on these repairs is to find a skilled, honest mechanic. Before you need repairs, look for a mechanic who:

1. is certified and well established;
2. has done good work for someone you know; and
3. communicates well about repair options and costs.

7.3.2. Insurance

Auto Insurance: You can save several hundred dollars a

year by purchasing auto insurance from a licensed, low-price insurer. Call your state insurance department for a publication showing typical prices charged by different companies. Then call at least four of the lowest-priced, licensed insurers to learn what they would charge you for the same coverage.

Talk to your agent or insurer about raising your deductibles on collision and comprehensive coverage to at least Rs. 50,000 or, if you have an old car, dropping this coverage altogether. This can save you hundreds of dollars on insurance premiums. Make certain that your new policy is in effect before dropping your old one.

Homeowner/Renter Insurance: You can save several hundred dollars a year on homeowner insurance and up to 2,500 a year on renter insurance by purchasing insurance from a low-price, licensed insurer. Ask your state insurance department for a publication showing typical prices charged by different licensed companies. Then call at least four of the lowest priced insurers to learn what they would charge you. If such a publication is not available, it is even more important to call at least four insurers for price quotes.

Make certain you purchase enough coverage to replace the house and its contents. "Replacement" on the house means rebuilding to its current condition. Make certain your new policy is in effect before dropping your old one.

Life Insurance: If you want insurance protection only, and not a savings and investment product, buy a term life insurance policy. If you want to buy a whole life, universal life, or other cash value policy, plan to hold it for at least 15 years. Cancelling these policies after only a few years can more than double your life insurance costs.

7.3.2.1. Banking/Credit

Checking Accounts and Debit Cards. You can save more than Rs. 5,000 a year in fees by selecting a free checking account or one with no minimum balance requirement. Request a complete list of fees that are charged on these accounts, including ATM and debit card fees. See if you can get free or lower cost checking through direct deposit or agreeing to ATM only use. Be aware of charges for using an ATM not associated with your financial institution.

Savings Products: Before opening a savings account, find out whether the account is insured by the federal government (FDIC for banks or NCUA for credit unions). Financial institutions offer a number of products, such as mutual funds and annuities, which are not insured.

Once you select a type of savings account, use the telephone, newspaper, and Internet to compare rates and fees offered by different financial institutions-including those outside your city. These rates can vary a lot and, over time, can significantly affect interest earnings. To earn the highest return on savings (annual percentage yield) with little or no risk, consider certificates of deposit (CDs) or U.S. Savings Bonds.

Credit Cards: To avoid late payment fees and possible interest rate increases on your credit cards, make sure you send in your payment a week to ten days before the statement due date. Late payments on one card can increase fees and interest rates on other cards.

You can avoid interest charges, which may be considerable, by paying off your entire bill each month. If you are unable to pay off a large balance, pay as much as you can. Try to shift the remaining balance to a credit card with a lower annual percentage rate (APR). You can find listings of credit card plans, rates, and terms on the Internet, in personal finance magazines, and in newspapers. Be aware that credit cards with rebates, cash back, travel awards, or other perks may carry higher rates or fees.

Auto Loans: To save as much as several thousand dollars in finance charges, pay for the car in cash or make a large down payment. Always get the shortest term loan possible as this will lower your interest rate. Make certain to get a rate quote (or pre-approved loan) from your bank or credit union before seeking dealer financing. You can save as much as Rs. 50,000 in finance charges by shopping for the cheapest loan. Make certain to consider the dollar difference between low-rate financing and a lower sale price.

First Mortgage Loans: Although your monthly payment may be higher, you can save tens of thousands of dollars in interest charges by shopping for the shortest-term mortgage you can afford. For each Rs. 5,000,000 you borrow at a 7% annual percentage rate (APR), for example, you will pay over Rs. 3,750,000 less in interest on a 15-year fixed rate mortgage than you would on a 30-year fixed rate mortgage.

You can save thousands of dollars in interest charges by shopping for the lowest-rate mortgage with the fewest points. On a 15-year Rs. 5,000,000 fixed-rate mortgage, just lowering the APR from 7% to 6.5% can save you more than Rs. 250,000 in interest charges over the life of the loan, and paying two points instead of three would save you an additional Rs. 50,000.

Check the Internet or your local newspaper for mortgage rate surveys, then call several lenders for information about their rates (APRs), points, and fees. If you choose a mortgage broker, make certain to compare their offers with those of direct lenders. Be aware that the interest rate on most adjustable rate mortgages (ARMs) can vary a great deal over the lifetime of the loan. An increase of several percentage points might raise payments by hundreds of dollars a month, so ask the lender what the highest possible monthly payment might be.

Mortgage Refinancing: Consider refinancing your mortgage if you can get a rate that is lower than your existing mortgage rate and plan to keep the new mortgage for at least several years. Calculate precisely how much your new mortgage (including points, fees and closing costs) will cost and whether, in the long run, it will cost less than your current mortgage.

Home Equity Loans: Be cautious in taking out home equity loans. The loans reduce or may even eliminate the equity that you have built up in your home. (Equity is the cash you would have if you sold your house and paid off your mortgage loans.) If you are unable to make payments on home equity loans, you could lose your home.

Compare home equity loans offered by at least four reputable lending institutions. Consider the interest rate on the loan and the annual percentage rate (APR), which includes other costs, such as origination fees, discount points, mortgage insurance, and other fees. Ask if the rate changes, and if so, how it is calculated and how frequently, as this will affect the amount of your monthly payments.

7.3.3. Housing

Home Purchase: You can often negotiate a lower sale price by employing a buyer broker who works for you, not the seller. If the buyer broker or the broker's firm also lists properties, there may be a conflict of interest, so ask them to tell you if they are showing you a property that they have listed. Do not purchase any house until it has been examined by a home inspector that you selected.

Renting a Place to Live: Do not limit your rental housing search to classified ads or referrals from friends and acquaintances. Select buildings where you would like to live and contact their building manager or owner to see if anything is available. Remember that signing a lease probably obligates you to make all monthly payments for the term of the agreement.

Home Improvement: Home repairs often cost thousands of dollars and are the subject of frequent complaints. Select from among several well established, licensed contractors who have submitted written, fixed-price bids for the work. Do not sign any contract that requires full payment before satisfactory completion of the work.

Major Appliances: Consult Consumer Reports, available in most public libraries, for information about specific appliance brands and models and how to evaluate them, including energy use. There are often great price and quality differences. Look for the yellow Energy Guide label on products, and especially for products that have earned the government's energy star, which can save up to 50% in energy use.

Once you've selected a specific brand and model, check the Internet or yellow pages to learn what stores carry the brand. Call at least four of these stores to compare prices and ask if that's the lowest price they can offer you. This comparison shopping can save you as much as Rs. 5,000 or more.

7.3.4. Utilities

Electricity: To save as much as hundreds of dollars a year on electricity, make certain that any new appliances you purchase, especially air conditioners and furnaces, are energy-efficient. Information on the energy efficiency of major appliances is found on Energy Guide Labels required by federal law.

Enrolling in load management programs and off-hour rate programs offered by your electric utility may save you up to Rs. 5,000 a year in electricity costs. Call your electric utility for information about these cost-saving programs.

Heating and Cooling: A home energy audit can identify ways to save up to hundreds of dollars a year on home heating (and air conditioning). Ask your electric or gas utility if they audit homes for free or for a reasonable charge. If they do not, ask them to refer you to a qualified professional. Enrolling in load management programs and off-hour rate programs offered by your electric utility may save you up to Rs. 5,000 a year in electricity costs. Call your electric utility for information about these cost-saving programs.

Telephone Service: Once a year, review your phone bills for the previous three months to see what local, local toll, long distance, and international calls you normally make. Call several phone companies which provide service in your area (including wireless and cable), to find the cheapest calling plan that meets your needs. Consider a bundled package that offers local, local toll and long distance, and possibly other services, if you heavily use all the services in the bundle.

Check your phone bill to see if you have optional calling features or additional services, such as inside wire maintenance, that you don't need. Each option you drop could save you Rs. 2,000 or more each year. If you make very few toll or long distance calls, avoid calling plans with monthly fees or minimums. Or consider disconnecting the service altogether and use dial around services such as 10-10 numbers or prepaid phone cards for your calls. When shopping for dial around service, look for fees, call minimum, and per minute rates. Treat prepaid cards as cash and find out if there is an expiration date.

If you use a cell phone, make sure your calling plan matches the pattern of calls you typically make. Understand peak calling periods, area coverage, roaming, and termination charges. Contracts offered by most carriers will provide you with a trial period of 14 days or more. Use that time to make sure the service provides coverage in all the places you will be using the phone (home, work etc.). Prepaid wireless plans tend to have higher per minute rates and fees but may be a better option if you use the phone only occasionally.

Before making calls when away from home, compare per minute rates and surcharges for cell phones, prepaid phone cards, and calling card plans to find how to save the most money. Dial your long distance calls directly. Using an operator to place the call can cost you up to Rs. 500 extra. To save money on information calls, look the number up on the Internet, or in the directory.

7.3.5. Others

Food Purchased at Markets: You can save hundreds of dollars a year by shopping at lower-priced food stores. Convenience stores often charge the highest price. You will spend less on food if you shop with a list, take advantage of sales, and purchase basic ingredients, rather than prepackaged components or ready-made items. You can save hundreds of dollars a year by comparing price-per-ounce or other unit prices on shelf labels. Stock up on those items with low per-unit costs.

Prescription Drugs: Since brand name drugs are usually much more expensive than their generic equivalents, ask your physician and pharmacist if a less expensive generic or an over the counter alternative is available. Since pharmacies may charge widely different prices for the same medicine, call several. When taking a drug for a long time, also consider calling mail-order pharmacies, which often charge lower prices.

Funeral Arrangements: Plan ahead, making your wishes known about your funeral, memorial, or burial arrangements in writing to save your family or estate unnecessary expense. For information about the least costly options, which may save you several thousand dollars, contact a local Funeral Consumer Alliance or memorial society, which are usually listed in the Yellow Pages under funeral services.

8

HOW TO INVEST MY MONEY

8.1. WAYS TO INVEST MONEY

8.1.1. Mutual Funds or Stocks

Stocks are shares of ownership in a company. You can buy shares through a brokerage at the price per share. Historically, the stock market has averaged annual returns per year of 11 percent. Of all the different types of investments, stocks will give you the most for your money. However, stocks can also be the most volatile. Risk and return go hand-in-hand. In the long run history has shown that financial markets recover, so stocks should be considered investments for the long run.

A mutual fund is a huge collected amount of money from a large group of investors that the mutual fund manager uses to buy lots of different stocks, bonds, and/ or other assets that meet the company's investment criteria. When you buy shares in the fund, you become a shareholder. When you give your money to the fund, you are giving your money to the expert money manager of the mutual fund. Mutual funds give you diversification and expert money management which allows you to sit back and relax. Mutual funds carry a low amount of risk. If you are a low risk taker, mutual funds may be for you. If you can't stand watching your money going up and down every day by large amounts, then invest in mutual funds.

Mutual funds are safe and low risk investments, because they diversify. They give your money a little taste of everything. The fund will invest your money in a number of different stocks in different industries. That way, a single company's depreciation can balance out with another company's appreciation. Mutual funds are generally good investments for retiring, saving for college, or any other goal that needs time. If you have some money that you don't need anytime soon, and don't want to take too much risk or spend time tracking your investment, then invest your money into a mutual fund.

However, mutual funds do have their disadvantages. The biggest disadvantage to know about a mutual fund is that most mutual funds underperform the stock market's average every year. 90 percent of mutual funds, in the last decade, have underperformed the market. Think about it, all those "expert" money managers can't even beat the market. "Mutual funds are boring!" That's what anxious investors who want to gain their wealth a little quicker say. They think of investing their money in stocks as an adventure and can live with price fluctuations, while they scowl at leaving their money in a snail speed mutual fund.

Both mutual funds and stocks can be for long term investors. But over the longer period of time, the stocks will prevail over the underachieving mutual funds. Those who cling too tightly to the familiar deny themselves many opportunities. There is no progress without risk.

8.1.2. Equity Investments Raising Money

Bringing investors into your business gets you more than just money — you get new co-owners, too. Unlike a lender — who temporarily provides you with money to operate your business — equity investors actually buy a piece of your business. For better or worse, they become your co-owners and share in the fortunes and misfortunes of your business. Here's a look at the pros and cons of raising money through equity investors and the different forms this equity investment can take.

As co-owners of your company, your investors will have some say in the way you run your company. They will probably be able to vote to elect your board of directors, and they have a legal right to be informed about all significant business events. And they can sue you if they feel their rights are being compromised. On the other hand, investors can bring helpful business experience with them that can strengthen your company. People who invest in your business may accept the risk of losing their entire investment and not insist that you guarantee repayment.

But to offset this risk, the investors may want to receive substantial benefits if the business is successful. For example, an investor may insist on a generous percentage of the business profits and, to help assure that there are such profits, may want to put a cap on your salary. The terms are always negotiable; there's no formula for figuring out what's fair to both you and the investor. In the end, you and your investors will have to work out what you are both comfortable with.

8.1.3. Investing the Cash Surplus

There are many investment opportunities available for your cash surplus. You must consider the advantages and disadvantages as well as the levels of risk, maturity, liquidity, and the yields of each of your investment opportunities. When investing a cash surplus, it's only natural to seek the highest rate of return for your investment. Four factors must be considered when making your investment decisions. Each factor plays an important role in determining the rate of return you receive on your invested cash surplus. These factors can also help you determine how much to invest and when to invest your surplus. These factors are given below:

8.1.3.1. Risk

The investment of your cash surplus should never be speculative — that is, high risk. As in most businesses, your cash surplus may only be a temporary surplus of cash inflows over your cash outflows. Any permanent losses resulting from a high risk investment could be devastating, even to the point of making you unable to continue your business. The level of risk you are willing to accept ultimately determines the yield of your investment. A higher level of risk will generally provide you with a higher yield.

On the other hand, a low level of risk will result in a lower yield on your investment. In some cases, you choose to invest in an investment with a higher level of risk to gain a higher yield. But as a rule, a conservative approach to the level of risk is recommended when investing your cash surplus.

8.1.3.2. Liquidity

Liquidity describes how easily you can access the cash you put into an investment. Some investments are more liquid than others. For example, investing your cash surplus in a money market account is very liquid. You can pull cash from a money market account when you need it without incurring any penalties for withdrawing the funds. Other investments offer less liquidity and have penalties for withdrawing early.

A CD (certificate of deposit) is an example of an investment that has this type of penalty if the CD is not held for its full term. When investing your cash surplus, be sure to consider the investment's liquidity. If the amount and duration of your cash surplus are uncertain, then you should consider only those investments that offer a high level of liquidity. On the other hand, if the amount of your cash surplus and the duration of the surplus are fairly certain, then less liquid investments should be considered. Preparing a cash flow budget should help you determine the amount and the duration of your cash surplus.

The liquidity of your investments also affects the yield of your investment. An investment that is highly liquid, such as a checking money market account, will generally result in a lower yield on your investment. On the other hand, an investment with a low level of liquidity, such as a CD, will generally provide you with a higher yield

8.1.3.3.Maturity

Maturity is the term used to describe the length or the duration of your investments. Many investments are made to be held over a certain period of time. An investment that is held for its full duration is said to have been held to maturity. When an investment has reached its maturity, the original investment and any gains or losses earned by the investment are returned to the investor. The maturities of your investments should occur so that the surplus cash is available when your business needs it. Preparing a cash flow budget is the best way for you to determine the appropriate maturities for your investments in light of your future cash inflows and outflows.

As a rule, you should try to stagger the maturities of your investments so that investments mature periodically. Investments that mature at a time when your business does not require the surplus cash can always be easily reinvested. The maturity of your investments has a direct impact on the yield of your investment. A longer maturity will generally provide you with a higher yield. On the other hand, an investment with a shorter maturity or no maturity at all will result in a lower yield on your investment.

8.1.3.4. Yield

Yield is the last factor to consider when making your cash surplus investment decisions. For most investments, the yield is determined by three other factors: risk, maturity, and liquidity. Once you've determined your acceptable level of risk, maturity, and liquidity, the type of investment and the yield of the investment are pretty much determined for you, or at least you've narrowed your options

8.1.4. Investment Fund Building

If you are like many small business owners — particularly those just starting out — you have a large portion of your personal assets invested in your business. This may be necessary and advisable now, but as your business develops, it will become prudent to branch out into more general and diverse investments as well. At some point, this will be true even if the additional income to be gained from continued heavy investment in your company would exceed the investment return that you could get on any "outside" investment. Presumably, one of the main reasons why you chose business ownership was to be able enjoy a certain standard of living and personal wealth.

As a small business owner, you probably look to the continued success and growth of your company to generate a major part of your personal income. Because of this, your business certainly deserves your main attention and priority — both in time and necessary working capital. Although an investment planning process such as ours will sometimes present you with the choice between allocating business profits back to the business, or to a more diversified portfolio, this planning process is aimed at doing the same thing for you that your business does: increase your personal wealth. This process will enable you, over time, to rely less on earned income, and more on unearned income.

The investment planning process itself doesn't in any way require you to retire or pull back from your business at any time; it does suggest that you should build the capability to do so, if you ever so desire. A diversified investment portfolio embodies that old saw that warns you against "putting all your eggs in one basket." By having several kinds of investments, such as stocks, bonds (government and corporate), real estate, and precious metals, you greatly reduce the chance that a particular economic or legal change will devastate your investment fund.

8.2. INVESTMENT GOALS

Many investors set their investment goals by set a targeted return that they want on their investments. Maybe they see this or that business commentator on TV saying that you shouldn't be content with less than X% return on your investment dollar. Or they get advice from a knowledgeable friend or business associate. A couple of problems can result from this targeted return approach.

First, unless an investor sets a targeted return based on established future goals, he or she may tend to overemphasise current, over long-term goals. Further, unless this investor has a firm idea of his or her personal risk tolerance, this may lead the investor to go after increasingly risky investments. The second potential problem with a return-based investment goal is that even if it is successful (that is, if the return figure is achieved), it won't give you all of the needed feedback to assure you that you will achieve your long-term goals. So, if you want to set current targeted return goals, you always keep a close eye on your continued progress toward reaching your larger personal financial goals.

8.2.1. Risk Tolerance Measurement

Generally speaking, the riskier an investment is, the higher it's expected return will have to be in order to entice investors. Determining how much risk to accept in your investment portfolio depends on two broad factors:

1. What are the inherent risks of the particular investment, and
2. How able and willing you are to deal with these risks (this factor is known as "risk tolerance").

Risk tolerance: When you evaluate the level of your personal risk tolerance, here are a number of things that you will want to consider:

1. *Family situation*: A stable marriage and good health may allow you to assume a bit more risk than if you are contemplating a divorce or separation or are experiencing the physical, mental, and economic effects of health problems.
2. *Age*: In general, the older you are, the less risk you may be willing to tolerate, since you are closer to the time when you may need to start living off your investment fund income (and possibly principal),

and have less time to overcome the impact of investment "mistakes."

3. *Business/employment situation*: A sufficient and stable stream of personal income provided by your business, outside employment, or spouse's income can go a long way toward giving you the flexibility to go for higher-return (and more risky) investments. For example, if your spouse has secure employment outside your business that provides a salary of Rs. 2,500,000, and employer-provided medical and retirement benefits, you might feel freer to go for more risky investments than you would if your business were the only source of your family's income.
4. *Debt and liquidity*: If you have a comfortably large fund of cash and other liquid assets to get you through a financial emergency, you probably will feel more prone to accept more investment risks than if you didn't have such a fund, or if you were burdened with a high level of debt.
5. *Other investments*: If you already have fixed-income and/or other conservative investments, you may be better suited to assume more risk than if you are currently heavily invested in high risk investments.
6. *Insurance*: Investment risk is not the only risk you face; you are confronted with risk of loss because of accident, ill health, disability, and premature death. If you have adequate insurance to indemnify yourself or your family on the occurrence of these risks, you have less of a need to have a large "self-insurance" fund of liquid assets. Because of this, you may feel free to move to higher return, higher risk investments.
7. *"Just you" factors*: This is last on the list, but certainly not least important. Despite what anyone

tells you about the safety and return of an investment, you have every right to take a pass on any investment that unduly raises your anxiety levels. No matter how safe an investment may be from an objective viewpoint, or how much income it may generate, you probably won't find it worth it if worrying about it threatens your health.

An investment plan can be beautiful on paper, but unless you put it into effect it won't help your financial security one bit. This brings us to a truth about investing: for every investor who fails to reach a goal because of making "bad" investments, there are several others who fail because they didn't invest at all. They had a plan that called for making systematic investments over a period of time, but somewhere along the line the planned investments were not made. Setting up an automatic investment plan, whereby you authorise funds to be withdrawn from a checking or savings account periodically for purpose of making pre-determined investments, can be a good way to go.

Although some investors may be wary of losing some degree of control over a portion of their income, this can be a way to make sure that you "pay yourself first." It is particularly important to guard against any tendency to procrastinate with respect to long-term goals, such as retirement. Depending on when you start investing to fund a retirement plan and how long these funds have to accumulate and grow, a delay of one year in starting the investment fund may mean of loss of Rs. 5,000,000 or more.

9

ART OF MAKING MONEY

The way you spend your money today will determine what you have six months from now, a year from now, five years from now, or in your lifetime. You control your financial destiny. You are responsible for the amount of money you earn and for the amount of money you spend. Successful money managers control the way they spend their money. They use money to accomplish the things that are important to them. Good money managers manage their money rather than letting it dribble away from them.

Do you have control of the way you spend your money? Do you live within your income, or do you have to borrow money or use savings to meet your regular monthly expenses? Living within your income requires careful planning. It requires self-discipline and the ability to say no to unnecessary spending. The ability to manage money has to be learned, developed, and practiced on a daily basis. There are eight steps to successful money management:

1. Get yourself organised.
2. Decide what you want to do with your money.
3. Look at all available resources.
4. Decide how much money you are worth.

5. Find out how much money you make.
6. Find out how much money you spend.
7. Set up a plan for spending your money and stick to it.
8. Evaluate your spending plan.

Following these eight steps will help you get control of your spending habits.

9.1. ORGANISED BUSINESS

Do you keep all of your bills and important papers in one location in your home? An organised business center will help you manage your family financial matters better. Keep all of your family records and business correspondence in one location. When you receive any bill or important letter from a creditor, put the correspondence in its proper place in your business center.

If you and a creditor disagree about how much you owe or the way you pay your bills, you have your own records to prove what has happened so far. Your business center may be elaborate or simple. The type of system doesn't matter as long as you have some way to organise your financial papers. Papers may be separated by using large envelopes or individual file folders in a file box or cabinet. Another alternative would be to use a three-ring notebook with dividers. Dividers with pockets could be used to store loose-leaf papers.

Label the dividers for your notebook or files according to the types of records you keep. For example labels might be tabbed as follows: net worth statement, record of earnings, record of expenditures, location of legal records, health records, real estate records, family papers, household inventory, employment records, automobile, housing, utilities, clothing care and information, credit card and installment payments, insurance, tax records, and general household information. Keep supplies needed for handling your business transactions in your business center. Keep envelopes, stamps, pens, pencils, checks, and a calendar at your fingertips to speed your monthly bill paying.

9.2. DETERMINE YOUR GOALS

What are some of the things you want to accomplish during your lifetime? Which of these costs money? You need to set up a plan for how you want to achieve these goals. Good money management begins with goal setting. Goals give you direction. They give you a purpose for the way you spend your money. Goals motivate and encourage you as you work toward doing things that are important to you. As an individual, you may have trouble deciding which item is more important than another. It's even harder when two or more people live together as a family unit and share money.

They may not agree on what is important. Because of this lack of agreement, it is sometimes hard to decide where money will be spent. Once you decide what is important to you, it will help you see what things you want to work toward. Goal setting involves more than deciding what's important to you. To help identify goals, ask yourself these questions:

1. What do I want to do with my money?
2. How much will it cost?
3. How long will it take me to get that much money?

When setting your goals, make a list. Take a pencil and piece of paper and write down what you want to do with your money. Make your goals very specific. Don't say, "I want financial security." Financial security is not very specific. Ask yourself what it takes to be financially secure. Your answer might be to have Rs. 1000,000 in savings when you retire in 20 years. Then you need to put Rs. 3098.50 a month for 20 years in a savings account that pays 3 percent interest. Your specific goal then is to save Rs. 3098.50 a month from now until you retire. This is a clearly defined goal.

Your goal should be realistic, challenging, and achievable. Is it possible for you to take Rs. 3098.50 out of your monthly budget and still meet your necessary living expenses? If you can afford Rs. 3,100 a month your goal is realistic, challenging, and achievable. If you can only afford to save about Rs. 1,550 a month, then you might have to reduce your long-term goal from Rs. 1000,000 to Rs. 500,000. Or you may want to look for an investment that will give you a higher rate of return than 3 percent. Goals should be measurable and reachable within a given time period.

Specify the date when you want to reach your goal. You can't put a date on reaching financial security, but you can save Rs. 1000,000 if you put Rs. 3098.50 each month in savings for 20 years. Your goals should be yours. Don't let someone else set your goals for you. You will be much more likely to reach your goal if it is something you really want to do. Goals are different for each individual and family. They change as you go through the different stages of life.

Once you set your goals, picture your goals in your mind. Creative daydreaming puts your goals into your subconscious mind. Once your dream is in your mind, you start thinking of ways to reach that dream. You automatically see ways to make your dream become a reality. Fix in your mind the exact things you want. Short-term goals are the things you want to get done in the next week, next month, in six months, or a year.

Intermediate goals are the things you want to get done in the next one to five years. Long-term goals are the things you want to do in the next five or more years. As you list your goals, decide which goals you want to use your money for first. As you set dates for reaching your goals, ask yourself which goals are the most important and which are the least important. Here are some questions to ask yourself as you decide which goal you will work toward:

1. How important is this to me and other family members?
2. How urgent is this? If today is April 14 and you owe Rs. 50,000 worth of taxes that is more urgent than paying off a Rs. 47,500 charge card debt.
3. What will happen if I don't work on this goal? If you owe a Rs. 35,000 credit card bill, paying it off Rs. 50,00 a month will cost you less money in interest than paying Rs. 1,750 a month. It may squeeze your budget to pay Rs. 5,000 a month, but it won't cost you as much money.
4. What will I need to reach this goal in terms of money, time, energy, skills, knowledge, and ability?

Goals are important keys to successful money management. Goals guide you so you use your money to do the things that are important to you. They can help you make your dreams come true within a specific period of time.

9.3. LOOK AT ALL AVAILABLE RESOURCES

To reach your goals, you'll need to look at all the resources available to you. They may include time, energy, skills, interests, knowledge, community services, or material goods. Public services such as the library, cultural events, health department, parks, and transportation facilities provide services and recreation for the family at little or no cost.

9.4. KNOW HOW MUCH MONEY YOU ARE WORTH

How much money are you worth? If you added up everything you own and subtracted everything you owe, would you own more than you owe? Or would you owe more than you own? Your financial net worth is determined by subtracting all you owe (your debts) from all you own (your assets). This information will be useful when determining your insurance needs, when applying for loans, when settling a divorce, or when planning your financial future. If you need to sell some assets to get cash to pay back debts, your net worth statement will let you see what assets you have and how much they are worth. Listed below are some guidelines to assist you in calculating your net worth:

1. Have a real estate agent estimate the current market value of your home or make note of the sale value of houses in your neighborhood.
2. Go on line to the Kelly Blue Book site to get the current market value of your car.
3. Have an expert appraise current market value of your furniture, antiques, art, jewelry, or other valuables.
4. Evaluate household items and electronics at what you would get if you sold them at a yard sale.
5. Check a newspaper or the Internet to estimate the current value of your stocks and bonds. s
6. Read your whole-life insurance policy to determine the cash value.
7. Determine the value of your pension plan. This would be the value if you stopped working at the present time.
8. Your net worth gives you an overview of your overall financial standing. Use your net worth

statement to help you plan for your financial future. Use it to help you identify financial goals you would like to work toward.

For insurance purposes get the appraised value of valuables in writing and ask the expert to sign the appraisal letter. These values need to be updated regularly. In addition, a general merchandise catalog can give you an estimate of the replacement value of other household items if you do not have the original sales receipts.

9.5. KNOW HOW MUCH MONEY YOU MAKE

How much money do you have to spend each month to meet basic living expenses and help you reach your goals? The money spent each month comes from various places. Money is usually obtained from one or more of the following sources:

1. Earnings from wages, salary, tips, or commission, rental income, interest, dividends, capital gains from the sale of an asset, or retirement benefits.
2. Money received from relatives, friends, or the government in the form of transfer payments such as social security.
3. Calculate Your Monthly Spendable Income
4. Find out exactly how much money you can spend each month.
5. Find your most recent pay stub.
6. Look at the amount of gross pay. Gross pay is the amount of money you earn before deductions.
7. Look at the amount of money going to each deduction. How much of your gross pay goes to each deduction (what percent)?

9. Look at the amount of your take-home pay. Your take-home, or net pay, is your gross income minus your deductions.
10. Look for your total spendable income. Total spendable income is your take-home pay plus money from other sources.
11. If you have an irregular income, estimate the total you expect to make for the entire year and divide by 12. Keep your estimate low. Workers such as salesmen, farmers, artists, and writers have irregular incomes.
12 Make a spending plan, a budget, for each month. Then when you get a check, spend it according to your budget. If you get an extra large check, stick with your original spending plan and put the extra in savings.

9.6. KNOW HOW MUCH YOU SPEND

How much money do you spend for food, housing, transportation, clothing, personal care, medical care, and other things? If you don't know how much you spend each month for these items, keep a record of your spending. Write down everything you spend every day for a month. When you make a purchase, write the amount down. The amount doesn't have to be exact, but close enough to help you see where your money is going.

After you have a written record of where all of your money is going, divide your spending into categories: fixed, flexible, and miscellaneous expenses. Spending can also be divided into daily, weekly, monthly, seasonal, or yearly expenses. Know what type of expenses you have. Know when and where you spend money so you can build a sound money management program. Fixed expenses are the budget items you pay a specific amount of money for every month for a certain period of time. These obligations are usually enforced through a signed contract.

Some examples are rent or mortgage payments, life insurance, car insurance, home insurance, and installment payments such as your car loan. Flexible expenses are the budget items you have more control over. You decide how much you will buy and how much you will spend. Flexible expenses include food, clothing, gas, electricity, water, phone, transportation, gasoline and car maintenance, personal care, medical expenses, furnishings, household expenses, education, and professional expenses.

Miscellaneous expenses are the extra items you purchase that may not be absolutely needed. Some miscellaneous expenses are snacks, tapes and CDs, reading materials such as magazines, and recreational activities such as the theater or movies. We're lucky that all our expenses don't have to be paid at the same time. We spend some money on a daily basis. We spend some on a monthly, quarterly, semi-annual, or annual basis. Then set aside enough money so you can cover an expense when it comes due.

Some examples of seasonal expenses are gifts, holiday meals, special occasions such as birthdays and anniversaries, back-to-school expenses, school trips, car repairs, property taxes, insurance (car, home, disability, life and health), license plates, and vacations and weekend trips. Monthly expenses may include house payment, car loan, and utility payments. Daily expenses include transportation and snacks.

9.7. STICK TO YOUR SPENDING PLAN

Once you have put a dollar figure on what you will spend each pay period, what can you do to make yourself stick to your spending plan? Before you spend your next dollar ask yourself these questions:

1. Will this purchase help me reach my financial goals? If your goals are important enough to you, they will motivate you to stick with your plan.
2. Is this purchase listed on my spending plan?
3. What will I have to give up if I spend my money on this purchase? Do I really need this new pair of shoes or do I need this money to buy groceries or gas for the car?

Make your new spending plan a part of your daily life. Use it as a guide to help decide where you can cut your expenses. For example, you may want to save Rs. 2,500 on your clothing expenses and put that money into savings. Look for ways you can spend less money. Start using your spending plan today. Don't put it off until tomorrow. Tell someone else what you're trying to do, so they can encourage you along the way.

Write down your new plan so it will be firmly planted in your mind. Don't let an exception get in the way of your new spending habits. If you start taking your lunch to work so you can cut food expenses, eating out one day will discourage your new habit and keep you from reducing your food bill. Stay away from tempting situations. However, remember that changing old habits takes time.

If you backslide into old habits, learn from the experience. What were the circumstances that led you to old habits? What can you do so that it does not happen again? Take advantage of every opportunity to break your old buying habits and encourage the new one. Continuously look for ways to reduce your spending. Do something every day that will help you save money. You may cut one coffee break at work. You may take your own instant coffee to work rather than buying coffee at the company cafeteria. Finally, develop a reward system for successfully following your spending plan. Choose a reward that will not sabtage your spending plan. If your reward will cost money, then save up to pay for it.

9.8. EVALUATE YOUR SPENDING PLAN

After you live with your spending plan a while, look it over. If you put Rs. 5,000 in savings at the first of the month and had to take out Rs. 2,500 before the end of the month, then maybe you can only afford to save Rs. 2,500 a month. That's okay. At least you know what you are able to save. Reviewing your spending helps you decide exactly how much you can spend or save. Review your spending plan regularly and revise it so it works for you. Here are some questions you can ask yourself as you spend your money.

Is this the best use of my money right now? Will this purchase help me reach my financial goals? Is there something else I need to use this money for? If you have trouble reaching your goals, you may want to reevaluate your goals. Are they really important to you? Is another family member or friend interfering with your ability to reach your goal? A sincere commitment and dedication to your spending plan can help you manage your money better.

SUGGESTED READINGS

Bonnie Runyan McCullough. (1996). *Bonnie's Household Budget Book: The Essential Workbook for Getting Control of Your Money.*

Bryce, Herrington J. (1987). *Financial and Strategic Management for Nonprofit Organizations*. Englewood Cliffs: Prentice-Hall.

Dara Duguay. (2001). *Please Send Money! A Financial Survival Guide for Young Adults on Their Own.*

David M. Schwartz. (1994). *If You Made a Million*. Mulberry Books.

Deborah McNaughton. (1999). *All About Credit: Questions (And Answers) About the Most Common Credit Problems.*

Gerri Detweiler, Marc Eisenson, and Nancy Castleman. (1999). *Slash Your Debt - Save Money and Secure Your Future.*

Golub, Holmer, McKiendall, Pohlman, Zenios. (1995). *"A Stochastic Programming Model for Money Management"*. European Journal of Operational Research.

Howard Strong. (1999). *What Every Credit Card User Needs to Know: How to Protect Yourself and Your Money.*

Ilyce R. Glink. (1999). *100 Questions You Should Ask About Your Personal Finances: And the Answers You Need to Help You Save, Invest, and Grow Your Money.*

John L. Macko, Jane E. Chidester. (1998). *BudgetYes! 21st Century Solutions for Taking Control of Your Money Now!.*

Judy Lawrence. (2000). *The Budget Kit: The Common Cents Money Management Workbook.*

Marsha Ludden. (1998). *Consumer Loans & Credit Cards: An Easy-To-Use Guide to Credit and Loans.*

Nancy Winslow Parker. (1995). *Money, Money, Money. Harper Collins.*

Oehler, John. (1996). *"Nonprofits must plan for success at raising money." Buffalo Business First, Buffalo:.*

Rex Johnson. (1995). *Guide to Home Budgeting*. The Anybody Can Do It.

Robert Hartzell Cole, Lon Mishler. (1997). *Consumer and Credit Management.*

Steven D. Strauss, Azriela L. Jaffe. (1999). *Complete Idiot's Guide to Beating Debt.*

Steven J. Schoeneck. (1996). *Making Ends Meet: How to Budget When You Don't Have Enough Money!*

Susan Abentrod. (1996). *10 Minute Guide to Beating Debt.*

William C. Wood, Downers Grove Ill. *Getting a Grip on your Money. InterVarsity Press.*